GOOGLE CLASSROOM

2020 EDITION: A STEP-BY-STEP PROFESSIONAL GUIDE FOR TEACHERS AND STUDENTS.

LEARN EVERYTHING YOU NEED TO KNOW TO USE GOOGLE DIGITAL CLASSROOM EFFICIENTLY.

MACARENA TORRES

TABLE OF CONTENTS

TABLE OF CONTENTS

INTRODUCTION

Google Classroom is a web service that was developed by Google for educators and schools to make assignments paperless, and to streamline the file-sharing system between students and teachers. Essentially, this uses the entire Google ecosystem, such as Google Docs, Slides, and Sheets for writing and presentation, the Gmail communication system, and for scheduling, you use Google calendar.

The coolest part about this is that if you do not want to talk on a computer or use a computer, there are mobile apps for both Android and Apple devices that let students do assignments on their device, even put photos on there, share different apps and files, and also access information on their devices, both online and offline. With this, teachers can contact and speak to students; they can monitor how a student is doing; and once they are graded, teachers can go back and add comments to their work, to ensure that students have the best education possible.

Essentially, this has made teaching way more productive, it also allows teachers to manage the coursework that is there. Everything is in one place, providing a more meaningful collaboration between both of these parties, and ensuring that students get the help that they need when the going gets tough.

The system allows more administrative tasks to be done effectively. Because of the G Suite for education, it makes tasks that are otherwise boring much faster. It works whether you are a teacher or a student; whether you use it from a computer or a mobile device.

It allows teachers to have access to the assignments that are there, the course materials they need, and all of the feedback in one place.

The coolest part about this is that it is free. It is free for schools that have signed up for G Suite for education and like with any of the tools the classroom. It meets the highest standards that are out there; it is a very fun system, and it is free and works better than most free software.

Another great thing about this is that it allows feedback to come back to the student right away. Educators can track the progress of a student and let them know how they are doing. More focus can be put on making sure that the student gets it, which is something that many students want to have. The cool thing about this is how integrative this is to the workplace for students, and teachers will be able to help in a much timelier manner. Plus, it allows for a more personalized construction, and it will allow students to have a better time learning subjects as well.

An increasing number of teachers are using the Google Classroom platform, which allows you to focus less on technology and more on teaching, as it allows you to organize a virtual classroom and distance lessons, without necessarily being a technology professional.

In this book, we will see all you need to get started with Google Classroom, and what it allows you to do. Next, we will see how to set up a class and create jobs such as assignments, quiz assignments, questions and provide teaching materials.

Each school has different sharing platforms, used websites and teleconference tools, which requires a mix of skills. Regardless of the technical means used, nothing comes close to the real classroom experience.

Whether you are a new teacher looking for something new to use with your students, or you are a teacher (who has been in the trade for a while) hesitant to use this system, anyone can take advantage of it. If you use this system, in the end, you will be able to create the best and most valuable system available.

How to Use This Guide?

Google Classroom: The Professional Guide Step-by-step for Teachers And Students To Learn Everything You Need To Know To Use Google Digital Classroom Effective And High Quality is the practical guide made for individuals who want to become virtual teachers. The steps and approaches in this guide are intended to provide a fundamental understanding of how to become an online teacher. This guide can be read in any order, and its practical framework should be used to start online instruction in your virtual classrooms.

This guide is ideal for people who are:

- New and experienced teachers, who want to switch to a virtual setting.

- Current virtual teachers, seeking additional help in their classrooms.

- Individuals interested in becoming virtual teachers and/or managing virtual classrooms.

- Practitioners and administrators, who want to make their online teaching experience more attractive to their audience.

What to Look Out For

This guide serves as a framework, as the field of online learning is expected to grow in the coming years. Those who are experts in the field should understand when and where to use the proposed material.

Google Classro...

CHAPTER - 1

BENEFITS OF GOOGLE CLASSROOM

For many educators, they may see that it is a great system, but who else can benefit from this? Well, let us talk about how it benefits everyone, including teachers, students, and parents. This chapter will tell you all about the benefits of Google Classroom for everyone, and why it matters.

Less Paperwork!

This is a benefit for everyone. Do you as a teacher tend to have worksheets that students may come to you days later to tell you that they lost it? Or maybe you need a new roll book for attendance? Or maybe you have this worksheet that you have found, but do not want to waste valuable class time trying to copy it? Or maybe you just do not want to deal with papers upon papers? If you are sick of it, then Google Classroom is for you. With this system, you can create worksheets in Google Drive, share them with the class, or even make a form for students to fill out. You can use the Share to Classroom feature to share new and valuable items to the classroom. Not only that, but you can also create a digital logbook, which in turn will save you lots of paperwork.

Allows the Use of Online Learning Platforms

One nice thing about Google Classroom is that it is so easy. For many students, when they get to college, they may be confused by the idea of online degree work. However, online classes are very popular, so if you want to get them ahead of the game, you should expose them to what it is like to have an online-only education. Google Classroom is a great way to do this, because it is very easy for everyone, and most students love it since everything is there.

Gets Better Conversations Going

Sometimes, it is very awkward trying to ask questions, and students are either too nervous to speak, or maybe they do not want to, or they often are explaining deep thoughts. But, did you know that you could get more engagement from students in a better way through the use of Google Classroom? Just posting a question in the questions area will get students to comment. The best part is other students can comment there, and it can deepen the way students do learn the coursework, and it can make your life easier. Even the most socially awkward of students will benefit from this, because it is easier to say things online, than in-person, and it can make a world of a difference in the long run.

Easy Support

One thing that is great about this, is that if you are a teacher or an administrator and do not know how to use this, you can get the help that you need. With G Suite, you will be able to use Google Classroom easily, with their helpful how-to software, set permissions, support at all times of the day. You actually can use this software and protect the data and classes. It is a secure software that really will help you and will ultimately really make your classroom easier to manage. The support can be direct with another person, or you can view some of the tutorials that you may be interested in, if you are looking to get better with this site and interface, this is ultimately the way to go. You can use a lot of different help tools to really benefit from this.

Can not Lose Work Anymore

If you are a teacher, chances are you have had to deal with the lost work excuses. Students lose work when it is on paper, or it involves a physical object. But, did you know that with this system, it eliminates the chances of you losing it? Since Google classroom eliminates the consumption of paper, so long as you have got access to the internet, you will be okay. Ultimately, it actually will save your district a ton of money on paper. It is quite nice, and it does the job.

Along with that, since it is cloud-based, no matter what computer you are on, you will be able to access your work. If you have everything on a cloud, it is based on an internet connection rather than a hard drive. You may have heard the excuse from a student that they had a hard drive failure, which is why they could not save it or turn it in. With Google Classroom, it actually can be accessed through all devices, and students can work wherever they are, and not worry about a flash Drive not being readable or losing work, and it eliminates the uses of constant emails. Plus, all the work saves to the Drive immediately, so if there is a computer hiccup, you do not have to worry about losing progress or anything. You do not have to hear the excuse that the computer crashed, or that they left the flash Drive at home since you are essentially going to be able to access everything through the internet.

Apps Galore

Google Classroom functions well on a mobile device, which means that you can take this on the go as well. Lots of times, students will make the excuse of they were not on the computer or did not see the assignment; but if they have a phone, they can download the application and get announcements and various assignments that are posted, to stay top of them. Teachers as well can post any of the assignments that they need in real time, through the application or the sharing support with this. It is very convenient and makes your life as a teacher that much easier.

Ease of Workflow

The nice thing about this is that with the interface, you can add on some products that sync with Google Classroom, and you can put extra add-ons and apps within this so that you have a full-on classroom environment. You can track the trends, users, and even students; administrators of the Google Classroom platform will give students and teachers a better platform over time. Plus, this is always updating, so you will have the support that you want to.

Real-Time Feedback

One thing that is very nice about this platform, is the fact that teachers can give feedback right away. With each assignment uploaded, the teacher can go through, make some notes, and then give the students feedback that they want. They can reach out immediately if the student is struggling, and work with them as needed.

Can Upload Resources

If you have students that need extra copies, you as a teacher do not need to worry about that. What you do, is upload the forms for assignments straight into Google Classroom, and from there, the students can take control over this. If a student misses an assignment, tell them it is in Google Classroom, and from there, you can have students check it whenever possible. It is quite simple.

Saves you SO Much money

One thing that is really nice about this, is the price of Google Classroom. It is free. It saves you a ton of money since everything is paperless and on a Drive. You can install free apps on this, to really help you get the most out of this, and you will be able to easily and without fail, create the lesson plans that you want, and the classroom you desire. It is quite nice, and you can differentiate all of these between classes too. Plus, with constant improvements, it is always growing.

Google Classroom is the future, and you will be able to easily and, without fail, make it better for every student. You do not have to worry about students falling behind; instead, you will be able to create a better learning environment that will make everything better.

CHAPTER - 2

SETTING UP GOOGLE CLASSROOM

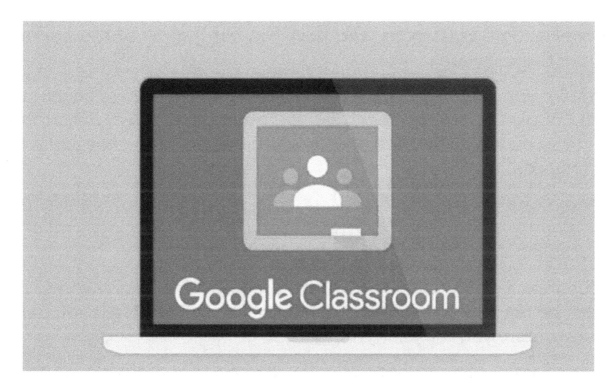

Creating an online education environment is easier these days, thanks to the development of Google Classroom. Gone are the days when this software was only available for educational institutions and G Suite accounts. Now, everyone can make use of Google Classroom.

One massive announcement was delivered in April 2017 by Google. This announcement made Google Classroom open and available to anyone with an active Google account.

As such, everyone can now benefit from the unmatched advantages of the Google Classroom platform. This simplifies the task of training, teaching, and planning of outreach to others, virtually.

If you own a business, you can now set up Google Classroom to interact with your customers, workers, team members, friends, classmates, etc. It goes without saying that Google Classroom is not just a useful tool; it is also effortless to operate.

In this chapter, I will introduce you to the steps involved in creating a new Google Classroom, and how you can get all of the benefits out of the software.

To start, you must ensure that you have an active Google account to use Google Classroom. Secondly, you must have a clear description of how you want the class and the setup to be, and what you want to focus on.

People often start with a test classroom, but creating your actual class requires more than creating a test class. All your ideas must be available before you proceed to create the class.

Your topics, materials to be used, assignments, class works, etc. must be ready before you can create the class. The idea is you being ready before you make anything.

Every class needs students, so you will need to invite them, and that can be done within the class. Well, it can wait till you are through with setting up the class.

Do not forget that creativity is so important when it comes to creating your online classroom. That will make the class more interesting. Engaging the students will make the class more interesting than it otherwise is.

With all these details in place, you are set to create your Google Classroom. Let us proceed with that right now.

Creating Your Google Classroom

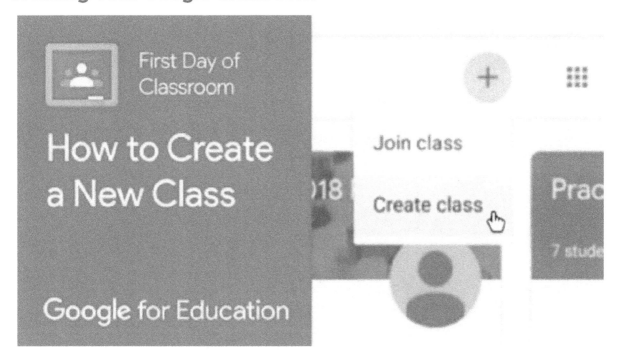

As stated earlier, it starts with opening a Google account. After that, you will proceed to the Google Classroom page, as depicted in the image.

From the Google Classroom page, click on the (+) button, and then select the Create Class option from the drop-down menu. You are expected to click the EULA checkbox, and select Continue. A page will pop up. From that page, you will need to assign a name to your class. You will also need to specify the section, and the subject you will be discussing.

Giving a Name to Your Class

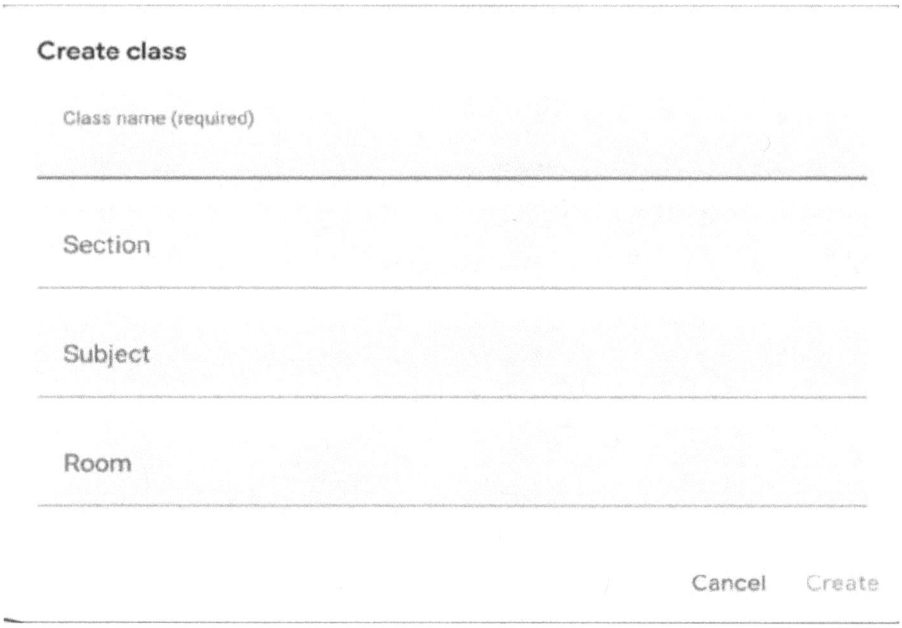

Create class

Class name (required)

_____

Section

_____

Subject

_____

Room

_____

Cancel   Create

After filling out all the information in the picture above, you can then click Create. As simple as that, you have created your class! Upon completing this, the next thing is to set up and customize the classroom.

Your class is ready!

You should get a message welcoming you to your class. There are several things to attend to on this page. We will highlight them all.

For a start, you will need to select a theme for your class. Click the Select Theme or Upload a Photo option to do this. Once you have picked the perfect look, it is time to write a description for the class.

That can be done by clicking the About tab on the screen and then selecting the option to do that in the next window. The dotted option should be clicked. There you will see the Edit option.

Click on it and enter the description for your class. You can add the meeting location and other details, as provided in the image below.

Creating the Class Description

When all the necessary information has been provided, click Save. If you are not teaching alone, you can then click on the Invite Teacher button and send invitations to other teachers to join you in the class. If you are teaching alone, you can skip this part.

Managing the class Drive folder is the next thing to do. The folder is where you will drop all class assignments and materials. You will update them to this folder and make them accessible to all your students. From Google Drive, you would have noticed that sharing permission is only for teachers.

You cannot and should not give this permission to students in your class. Students should only be able to access their assignments and materials from this file.

Many prefer creating a subfolder for assignment and material purposes. You can also create a subfolder for teachers where their material will be kept.

Creating a subfolder is very easy: navigate to Google Drive, click on the Classroom folder, and open it. You can then select the option Create A New Folder inside the classroom folder.

How to Create Assignments

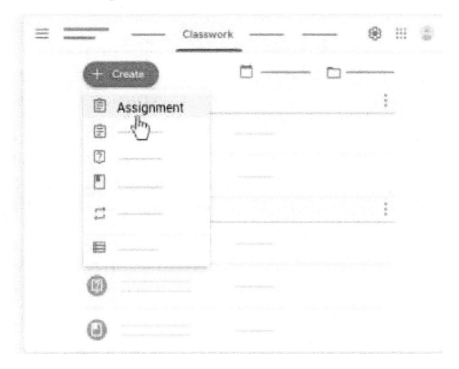

Your class should be ready at this point. Click on the Stream tab and click the (+) button located at the bottom right corner of the page. You will get a pop-up (picture below), and from there, you can create your announcement, assignments, ask questions, or manage previous posts.

How to Send Invites to Your Students

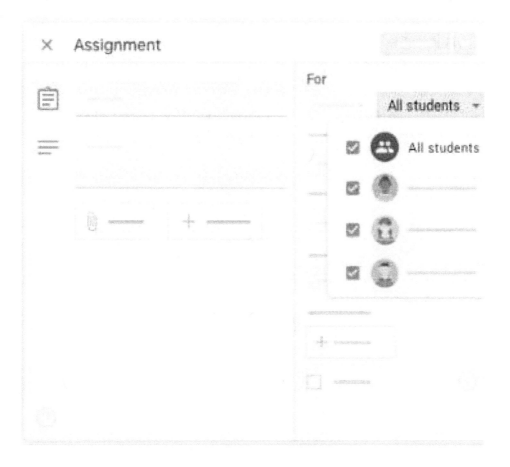

After setting everything up, you need students in your class. So, sending out invites to them is the next thing.

To do this, click on the Student tab and click the Invite Students button. If the students are in your Google contacts, you can invite them by name or email address.

There is a class code that you can also use to invite students. The code is delivered in the Student tab. If you have a list of students, you can send the class link and code to them via email. Upon joining the class, they can start to work on their tasks and interact with other students.

There is no easier way of creating an online class than this method. It is perfectly designed by Google, with incredible features that make it perfect for all teachers.

How to Create a Training Module

Organization is one of the essential things to get right when making use of Google Classroom for professional development. With modules, you can save time and help your employees become more engaged in the training. Upon completing the basic setup of the classroom, creating the training module is essential.

To do this, click on the (+) in classwork to enable you to create a new topic. Name this topic as appropriate.

The image below shows a classroom with the title "Professional Development & Training," and the training topic is "Differentiated Instruction." This will be the first module.

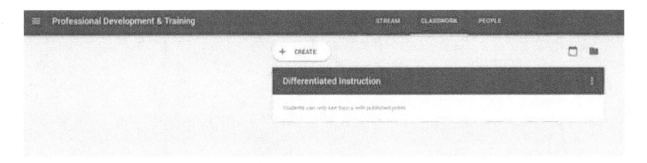

Adding Content to Your Module

Adding assignments and questions is straightforward, yet this critical feature relies solely on the ability to create engaging questions. Employees will become more engaged in the discussion when you add questions.

You can include files and content forms like slides from your Google Drive when adding an assignment. You can also include links to material or videos in the assignment.

As such, you can incorporate numerous learning styles for your employees and improve their engagement, while also making the learning process enjoyable.

It is important to set a timeline for completing the task; this will help each learner move at a defined pace that suits them while handling their tasks effectively.

Application for Google Classroom

There are numerous applications offered online, but they do not all work with Google Classroom. Most of the compatible ones are listed on the Google for Education Partners page list, and you can also find more by searching for #withClassroom on Google.

Using the Notification Feature in Google Classroom

One of the best ways to stay up to date regarding information about Google Classroom is through the notification feature. By default, both mobile and email notifications are turned on for teachers and students.

The type of device a student uses, and the kind of user will also affect the sort of notification received. However, there are lots of things you can adjust and personalize.

How to Access the Notification on Your Computer

Navigate to Google Classroom, and click on the triple bar menu located at the top left corner to access the Classroom main menu. Click the setting gearwheel to personalize the notification options.

How to Access the Notification on Your Device

Open the classroom application, then go to the main menu by clicking on the triple bar menu located at the top left corner. Click on Settings, and then select Notifications. You can personalize from this point.

Notification Option for Teachers

The notification for teachers is divided into several categories: comments, email, class notification, and classes the teacher takes. The email option allows you to switch email notifications on or off.

The comment option also allows you to receive notifications when a comment is made on your post by your students, or when you are mentioned in a comment.

If you turn off notifications, all categories of notification will be shut off automatically. Under the Class You Teach section, you can set notifications for assignments that are submitted later than expected, or when a student resubmits an assignment.

You can also receive the invitation to co-teach another class, and also see the status of your scheduled post. You can turn the notification for each class on or off only with your computer, as it is not available on mobile devices.

Notification Options for Students

The notification option for students is closely related to that of teachers. However, for students, the options are numerous. They can set notifications to know when the teacher posts an assignment, makes an announcement, returns their assignment, submits their grading, etc.

Whenever they receive an invitation to join a class, they will also get notified, and they can set due-date reminders for their assignment. Students can also personalize their notification options, and they can select the classes they want to receive notifications through their system.

Before you begin training in your class, ensure that everything is in place. Make use of appropriate titles that support what you offer. If several topics are addressed, create a different classroom for them.

Many have found it beneficial to set up their classes in such a way that different topics are grouped into specific learning modules. You can invite directly or share the code with your employees to join the classroom.

CHAPTER - 3

HOW TO CREATE AND MANAGE A CLASS

Classes are fun to create, and in this chapter, we will go over how you create a class, organize and manage the class, and remove classes once they are done. Classes are the most important aspect of this, since it is where everyone will be, and if you know how to put all of this together, you will be well on your way to a successful result with Google Classroom.

How to Create a Class

Now, once you have logged in it is time to create a class. When you first log in, you will get the option of either student or teacher. Always make sure that you indicate that you are the teacher, and if you mess up, you need to contact the administrator to reset it. It is very important, because students are limited in their options compared to teachers, and it can be quite frustrating. Now, if you are a student, you simply press the (+) button when you get it, to join a class. Teachers need to press Create a Class.

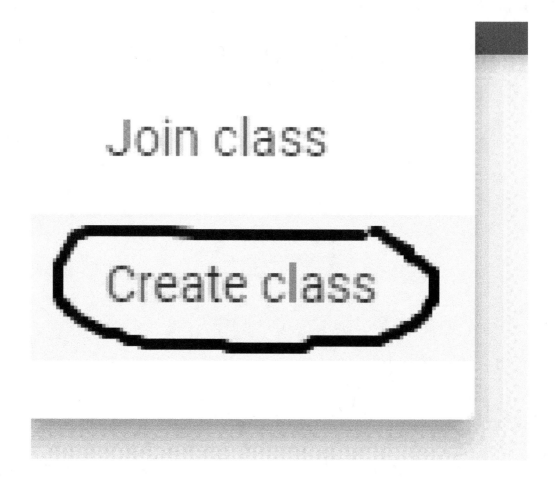

Now, if you have already got classes, chances are you will see some other names there. They will be displayed on the screen itself. Every time you press the plus button, you will then be able to add more.

Next, you are given a class dialogue boss. You will then type in the name and the section for this. You will be able to create the class immediately from here.

If you want to add more to it, you can go to the About tab, choose the title of the course, along with the description, location, and materials here. You do need to have a name for the class itself since this is how students will find the class when they open it up. If you have classes with multiple names on it, you will definitely want to specify either via time or day, especially if you have got a lot of sections. The Section field is how you do this, and you can create a subject as well, based on the list of subjects they provide for you.

Some teachers like to make these very descriptive, and you should ideally add as much information as you feel is needed for it. But do remember to make sure it is not some wall of text, that students will read and get confused by. As a teacher, you should make sure you do this in a way that students will get the information easily, and that they can delineate each class. It is also important to make it easy for your own benefit.

How to Manage a Class

The first thing that you can do when changing the class and managing it, is to give it a theme. One thing you will notice is that you do not have students in there as soon as it is created, so you can have a bit of fun with it. On the right side near the header of the class is a button by which you can change the class theme. You can use the themes that are provided. Some photos of the classes are good options, and you can use different templates for each one. This way you know exactly what theme you are using because they can sometimes be a bit complicated.

How to Remove, Delete and View a Class

When using Google Classroom, sometimes you will want to delete a class when it is the end of the semester, and you can always restore it again if you need to. You can also delete it if you either never want to see that class again or have no use for it because you have got the assignments already. Now, if you do not archive these, they will stick around, so make sure that you archive them first.

Archived classes essentially mean that they are in an area where you have the same materials, posts, and work the students have. You can view it, but you cannot actually use it, and it is good if a student wants the materials.

Archiving classes is simple to do. You choose the class, click the three-dotted button, and presto! It is archived.

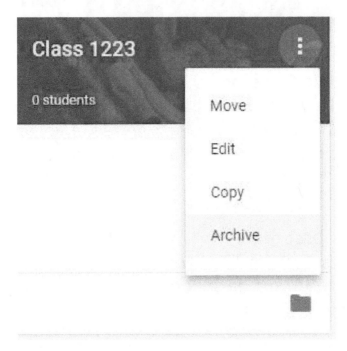

Now, to view an archived class after it is been archived, you press the three-lined button again, go down to the tab Archive Classes, and then choose the class you want to see.

To delete a class though, you essentially need to do the same thing. Remember, that you need to archive the class before you can delete it. Scroll all the way down, choose Archive Classes. From there, you need to press the three-dotted option, and then choose Delete This. From there, you will have the class fully removed. Remember though, you cannot undo this once you have done it, and if you do choose to delete a class, you do not have access to the comments or the posts. However, if you have any files that are in the Drive, you can always access those, since you have those in the class files themselves.

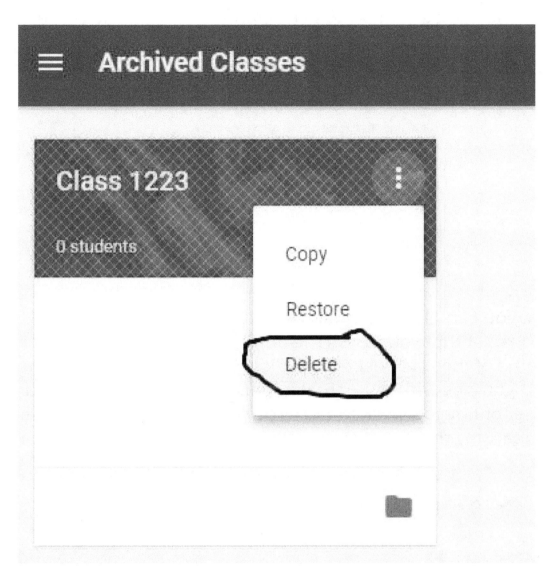

Other Tips and Tricks for Class Management

There are a few class management things that you can implement, and some tips and tricks that go into Google Classroom. The first thing that happens, is that when you get to the Classes tab, and you want to drag and move the classes around, you can do so. This is a good way to change the order of things, and it is quite easy to do.

Another important thing to remember is that you have the Classroom function. It is quite handy, and if you want to change the calendar or view it, you can essentially press the icon of the calendar and check it out to see what is coming up for every single class, because some classes may do certain things at different times of the semester.

Finally, you can always adjust the settings at any point. This is done with the gear that you see on the home screen. Here, you can change the name of the class, especially if it is confusing, and show the class code if you need it. You can also decide on the stream, and show whether or not you want items to be deleted or displayed. There are other features there too, and it is all right there waiting to be used.

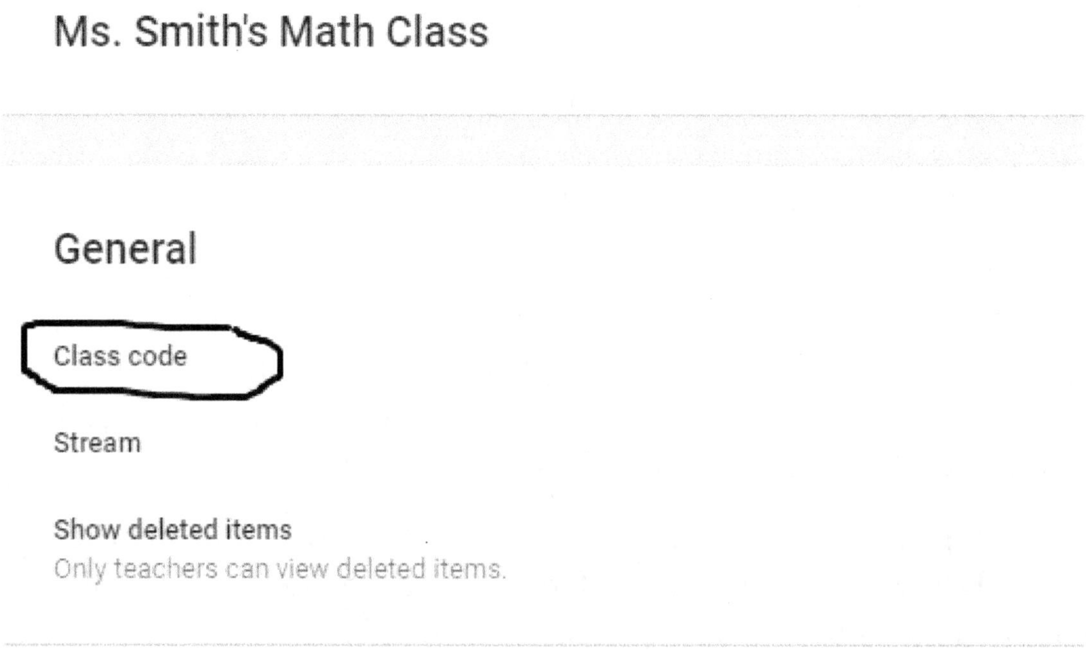

Ms. Smith's Math Class

General

Class code

Stream

Show deleted items
Only teachers can view deleted items.

When it comes to Google Classroom, knowing how to create the classes is a big part of it. If you have classes that you want to add, or you want to get started with Google Classroom, this is the way to go, and it is the surefire way to success.

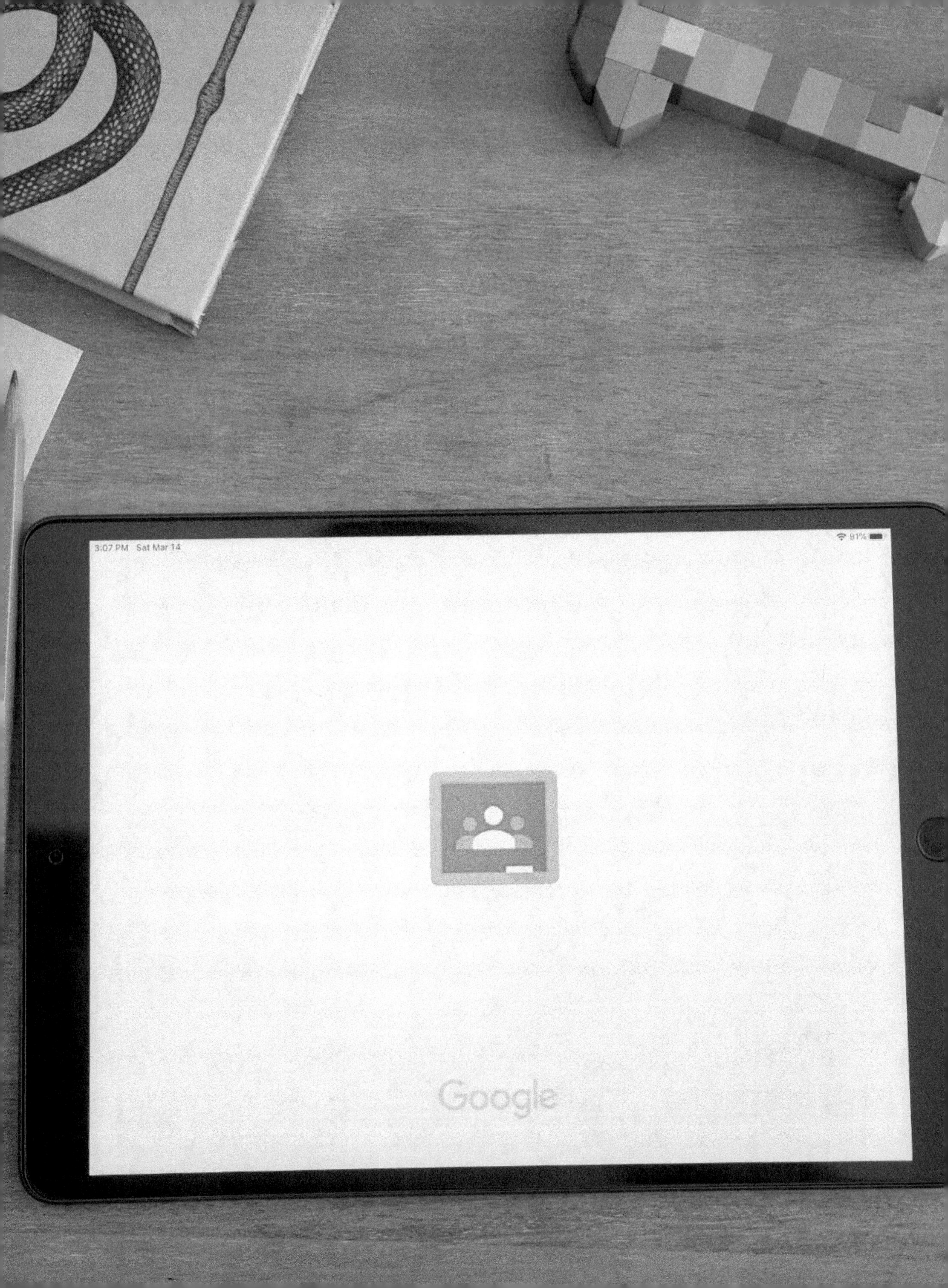
3:07 PM Sat Mar 14
91%
Google

CHAPTER - 4

HOW TO SET DUE DATES, MANAGE HOMEWORK, AND ASSIGNMENTS

Overview

Assignments are a useful tool on Google Classroom for delivering, tracking, and also grading student submissions. Even submissions that are non-electronic can also be tracked using the Assignments tool.

Add an Assignment

Creating an Assignment

- Open www.classroom.google.com.

- At the top, click on Class, and open Classwork.

- Also, click on Create and click on Assignment.

- Input the title and necessary instructions.

Posting Assignment

1. To one or more classes:

- Just below for, click the drawdown on Class.

- Choose the class you want to include.

2. To individual students:

- Select a class and click the drawdown on All Student.

- Uncheck All Students.

- Then select the particular student(s).

Inputting Grade Category

- Click the drawdown on Grade Category.

- Select Category.

Edit the following (optional):

- Click Grades to edit the grades page.

- Click Instructions to compose the Assignment.

- Click Classwork to create a homework assignment, a quiz, or a test.

Change the Point Value

- Click the drawdown below points.

- Create a new point value or click ungraded.

Edit Due Date or Time

- Click on the drawdown below Due.

- Click on the dropdown on No due date.

- Fix the date on the Calendar.

- Create due time by clicking Time. Input time by adding AM or PM.

Add A Topic

- Click on the drawdown below Topic.

- Click on Create Topic and input the topic name.

- Click on an existing topic to select it.

Insert Attachments

File

- Click on Attach.
- Search for the file and select it.
- Click Upload.

Drive

- Click on Drive.
- Search for the item and click it.
- Click Add.

YouTube

- Click on YouTube.
- Type in the keyword in the search bar and click search.
- Select the video.
- Click Add.

For Video Link URL

- Click on YouTube and select the URL.
- Input the URL and click Add.

Link

- Click on Link.
- Select the URL.
- Click on Add link.

You can delete an attachment

- Click removes or the cross sign beside it.

Add a Rubric

You must have titled the Assignment before you create a rubric.

- Click the Add sign beside Rubric.

- Click on Create rubric.

- Turn off scoring by clicking the switch to off, besides the Use scoring.

- Using scoring is optional; click Ascending or Descending, beside the Sort the order of points.

Note: Using scoring, gives you the room to add a performance level in any with the levels arranged by point value automatically.

- You can input Criterion like teamwork, grammar, or citations. Click the criterion title.

- Add criterion description (optional). Click the Criterion description and input the description.

Note: You can add multiple performance levels and criteria.

- Input points by entering the number of points allotted.

Note: The total rubric score auto-updates as points are added.

- Add A level title, input titles to distinguish performance level, e.g., Full Mastery, Excellent, Level A.

- Add a Description, input expectations for each performance level.

- Rearrange Criterion by clicking More and select Up or Down.

- Click Save on the right corner to save the rubric.

Reuse Rubric

- Click on the Add sign beside Rubric.

- Click Reuse Rubric.

- Enter Select Rubric and click on the title. You can select a rubric from a different class, by either entering the class name or by clicking the drawdown and selecting Class.

- To view or edit the rubric, click on Preview, and click on Select and Edit to edit. Save changes when it is done. Go back and click Select to view.

View Rubric Assignments

- Click on Rubric.

- Click the arrow up down icon for Expand criteria.

- Click the arrow down up icon for Collapse criteria.

The grading rubric can be done from the Student work page or the grading tool.

Sharing a Rubric

This is possible through exporting. The teacher creates the rubric exports, and these are saved to a class Drive under Rubric Exports. This folder can be shared with other teachers and imported into their assignment.

The imported rubric can be edited by the teacher in their Assignment, and this editing should not be carried out in the Rubric Exports folder.

Export

- Click on Rubric.

- Click More on the top-right corner and enter Export to Sheets.

- Return to the Classwork page by clicking close (cross sign) at the top-left corner.

- At the top of the Classwork page, click on the Drive folder and enter My Drive.

- Select an option, to share one rubric, right-click the Rubric. To share a rubric folder, right-click on the folder.

- After right-clicking, click on Share and input the e-mail you are sharing to.

- Then click Send.

Import

- Click on the Add sign beside Rubric and enter Import from Sheets.

- Click on the particular rubric you want and click on Add.

- Edit the rubric (optional).

- Click on Save.

Editing Rubric Assignment

- Click on the Rubric.

- Click on More at the top-right corner and enter Edit.

- Click Save after making changes.

Deleting Rubric Assignment

- Click on Rubric.

- Click on More at the top-right corner and enter Delete.

- Click Delete to confirm.

Posting, Scheduling or Saving Draft Assignments

Post

- Open Classwork and click on Assignment.

- Click on the drawdown beside Assign, on the top-right corner.

- Click on Assign to post the assignment.

Schedule

- Click on the drawdown beside Assign, on the top-right corner.

- Enter Schedule.

- Input and the date you want the assignment posted.

- Click Schedule.

Save

- Click on the drawdown beside Assign, on the top-right corner.

- Enter Save Draft.

Editing Assignment:

- Open Classwork.

- Click on More (three-dotted button) close to Assignment and enter Edit.

- Input the changes, and save for posted or schedule assignment, while Go to Save draft, to save the draft assignment.

Adding Comments to Assignment

- Open Classwork.

- Click Assignment and enter View Assignment.

- Click on Instructions at the top.

- Click on Add Class Comment.

- Input your comment and post.

To Reuse Announcement and Assignment

Announcement

- Open the class.
- Select Stream.
- Slide into the Share Something with Your Class box, and click on a squared, clockwise up and down arrows, or Reuse post.

Assignment

- Open Classwork and click on Create.
- Click on a squared, clockwise up and down arrows or Reuse post.
- Select the Class and Post you want to reuse.
- Then click on Reuse.

Delete an Assignment

- Open Classwork.
- Click on More (three-dotted button) close to Assignment.
- Click on Delete and confirm it.

Creating a Quiz Assignment

- Open Classwork and click on Create.
- Click Quiz Assignment.
- Input the title and instructions.

You can switch to Locked Mode on Chromebooks, to ensure students cannot view other pages when taking the quiz.

You can switch on Grade Importing to import grades.

Response and Return of Grades

Response

- Open Classwork.

- Click on Quiz Assignment, and free Quiz Attachment.

- Click on Edit and input Response.

Return

- Open Classwork.

- Click on Quiz Assignment.

- Pick the student and click on Return.

- Confirm Return not to score a task.

Evaluating and Returning Assignments to Students

Educators can discover student entries in various manners. Be that as it may, maybe the most productive route is to enter the class you are keen on evaluating and tapping on the task name from the Stream page. When you find that assignments are getting covered among student discussions, take a look at the sidebar on the upper left of the Stream view, and you should see the Up and Coming Assignments box. Click on the task you need to review and follow the bearings underneath:

1. Click the name of the student who has presented a task you need to review.

2. When the report opens, utilize the remarking highlights in Drive to leave point-by-point input on explicit pieces of the student accommodation. Close the archive when you are finished. All progressions are spared consequently.

3. When you come back to Classroom, click to one side of the student's name, to No evaluation, and enter a focused-based evaluation for the task.

4. Check the container close to the student you simply reviewed, at that point click the blue Return button, to save the review and inform the student that their paper has been evaluated.

5. Add any new criticism in the spring up box. At that point, click Bring Assignment Back.

Evaluating: Tips and Further Information

How do the students realize that you have evaluated their task? Do you need to review a task out of 100? These inquiries are answered below.

- When the educator restores a task to a student, the instructor no longer has altering rights on that record.

- You can restore a task to a student without reviewing it, by just checking the case close to the student's name and clicking Return. This could be valuable for assignments submitted in blunder.

- When you return a task to a student, they will naturally get an email warning advising them regarding your activities

- You can change an evaluation whenever by tapping on the review and afterward clicking Update.

- Clicking the envelope catch will open the Google Drive organizer where all student entries are put away. This helps check on all the submitted assignments one after another.

The default number of focuses for a task is 100. However, you can change this by tapping the drop-down bolt and choosing another worth, composing your very own estimation, or in any event, picking the choice.

CHAPTER - 5

HOW TO GRADE ASSIGNMENTS AND THEN PUT THEN ON GOOGLE SHEETS

Quality Tests and Quizzes With Google Forms Automatically

If you ever wanted your Scantron program to identify basic answer tests and quizzes for you automatically, you are lucky: Google Forms has a function.

Login into Google Form with your Google account to create a test/ quiz in Google Forms and click on Template List. Scroll down, and a portion of educator type templates will be shown. Choose Quiz blank.

Create A Questionnaire Using Google Forms

Using this template, multiple-choice, checkbox, or download quizzes and tests can be generated, distributed, and automatically graded. You may also pick what test participants see during the contest; you can control private scores or let students know if they got the answer right now.

Create a Google Formula Test

You need to create the quiz and response keys in Google Forms to use Google Forms to automatically rate your quizzes and tests. To construct your questionnaire, follow the following steps:

- To add a question to the quiz, press the (+) button.

- Using the menu to pick a question (short answer, multiple-choice, checkbox, dropdown, etc.) that you are curious about.

- Type your question and any response options, if appropriate.

- If you need explanations or examples, add photos or videos to the post.

Request Settings Adjustment

Repeat each move you want to add to your quiz above for each question. When finished, click Send and change the settings of your quiz.

Specific Configurations:

If you want your students to enter a printed confirmation that they have completed the quiz, check the boxes next to collect email addresses and responses.

If you want your school students to take a test from their Google Accounts provided by the school, check the box next to the Restrict to Users in [a domain in your school] and trusted domains.

If you do not want students to take the quiz more than once, check the box next to Limit to 1.

Settings for Submission:

Check the box next to Show Progress Bar, to see a visual indicator that shows how many more questions students need to respond to.

Check the box next to the Question Order Shuffle if you want to answer questions from all your students randomly.

In the message box, customize the text. This is the text that shows how the students do the exam and is a good place for memorabilia, such as, "Turn this page tomorrow morning and make sure you print it."

Settings for Quizzes

Choose whether or not students will be assessed directly after each submission, or after a manual examination, by clicking the radio button next to each submission.

When you want students to figure out what questions they answered incorrectly, check the box next to the missing questions.

Check the box next to Right answer if you want to see students after grading their quiz.

Check the box next to the Points value if you want students to see how many points a question is worth.

Settings for the quiz in Google Forms Adjust

Send your questionnaire and gather results.

Tap Send again when you save your settings. Consider how you want to submit the contest to the students: you can email it, create the customized URL of the contest, or post the full content on your website. If you send the questionnaire via email, enter the email addresses of your students, and click Send.

Upon completion of the exam, go back to the contest to see the grades for each subject. You can type this manually into your Gradebook software or click the tab to send your questionnaire to a Google Sheets gradebook, either new or existing.

Export to Web Sheets Google Forms Questionnaire Scores

Gather Valuable Information with Google Sheets And Measure Ratings

If you are using Gradebook software, your school will probably calculate grades for you – just enter the grades and the weights of the assignment in your system. Google Sheets simplifies the process of tracking and calculating student grades if your school has invested in Gradebook software.

Build A Gradebook for Google Sheets

You do not need help with setting up complicated formulas for you to measure and weigh classifications if you are a master spreadsheet user and know how to quickly construct formulas. If you do not know the structure of the Table, but you can use the Gradebook for Google Sheets and the Classroom add-on if you want a method that lifts the heavy for you.

To build a book with the add-on of Gradebook, do the following:

Browse Google Sheets and create a new, blank tablet.

Choose Add-ons and choose to Get add-ons.

Type 'Gradebook' into the search bar, click Enter for Google Sheets & Classroom.

To install the add-on, please click Free in the Gradebook row for Google Sheets & Classroom.

Use the Google account with the add-on that you want to use.

Check and approve the permissions needed.

Upon finishing your installation, click the Add-ons button again in your Google Sheet, hover to Gradebook, and select Creating and Viewing Gradebooks. When you have completed the installation, click again. When the system is completed, a new window opens to the right of your chart. Using it to set up the current classifications:

To set the calculations for weighting assignments, automatically pick a form of the Gradebook.

Enter your course name and click Join.

Fill in any other information you wish to include in your gradebook.

To start, press the Creating Course.

Make a Google Sheets gradebook

Click on the link to open your new gradebook at the top of the Gradebook sidebar of the course. Your gradebook Google Sheets is opening in a new window.

First, you must set your classes and weighted percentages in the Settings tab of the new Google Sheets gradebook, if you calculate grades by weighting assignments in different categories.

Creating Gradebook for Google Sheets Weighted Categories

Now, you simply must include each student in the Gradebook sheet in its row, add your tasks, categories, and job details. When you finish graduating, add grades to your students, and Gradebook calculates the grades for you automatically.

Sheets & School Gradebook for Google

Price: Free for any features in google sheets.

Google Sheets & Classroom Gradebook: $18 / year for the premium add-on, which makes exports to Google Docs or PDF of course reports.

Gain Valuable Information on The Exploration Role Of Google Sheets

Hiding at the bottom of every Google sheet is an exploration tool that helps you to access data in your book and gain valuable insights.

Google Sheets Exploration Option

To track student progress or test results easily use the Explore option. Since it is automatic, you can gain insights that you may not have been thinking about requesting.

Let us say that in your course or test, you want to find an average grade. Rather than finding it out, learning instinctively would do it for you. Columns, columns, or data clusters you wish to collect, highlight the gradebook, and click Explore.

Google Sheets Explorer measures average grades.

The Explorer feature produces numerous graphs and visuals of your results, which can be transferred to the tablet.

Data visualization for Google Sheets

Finally, you can insert your data into the Explore Answers box if you have questions about your data. A great time-saver can use the natural language to ask questions instead of formulas (for example, "Which person has the highest score?"). If, for instance, Column Z in the following screenshot says "Grade" rather than "Performance," I would ask, "Which student is of the highest grade?"

Tell a Google Sheets Explore query.

Success with Google Docs Class Papers

By using Google Docs, it is easier for students to avoid certain excuses to avoid late work penalties, by having their papers electronically submitted; 'the printer broke' excuse will not be able to cut it. Also, students who use a sneaky font or strange line spacing do not need to worry about transforming four-page papers into five-page papers; also, you can see exactly what fonts and formats they have been using.

However, Google Docs is much more helpful than keeping your requirements under control. It can also be utilized by teachers to check facts and plagiarisms, propose copy edits, leave comments, and review previous drafts.

Google Docs Discovery Feature

A menu will appear on the right of the document when you click Explore. Use it to scan the web as you want on Google; it automatically retrieves suggestions for analysis, photos, and web content.

Click Browse. Type in a search bar a subject or copy and paste the text directly from your report to check evidence or plagiarism in your grading papers. For that specific text, you will receive analysis, article, and picture suggestions.

No Google Docs search the web.

If a student has an unknown reality, use Explore to quickly scan the website and test its accuracy.

Explore is particularly useful when you think a student has plagiarized (or all) material of your paper. Copy and paste a questionable sentence and Explore will compile tests for any online material with the same words.

Google Docs Exploring Plagiarism

Offer edits for copies of the articles and leave comments.

Google Docs' provocative mode enables you to suggest editing copies of student papers easily – no red pen is required. Click on the icon and turn to Suggest mode after you open a student paper. Now, when it is time to rewrite this article, you will recommend improvements to your students.

Google Docs Feature Recommendation

You may also leave notes on items to be reviewed, changed, or deleted by students. Click the comment icon to add a comment in that copy section and highlight the respective text.

Google Docs Adds A Statement

Examine past drafts of student records

This makes it simpler if students write their comments in the previous drafts, but some still seem to lose track and forget to turn on earlier drafts. That is no longer a problem with Google Docs.

Google Docs saves copies of each revision made to the document so that the revisions you request are easy to see. To order to see the exact improvements made by the students, you can even equate prior versions with current versions.

CHAPTER - 6

INNOVATIVE TOOLS THAT ENHANCE LEARNING

With Classroom, Google is entering an effectively competitive market, ready with powerful learning administration frameworks. Where it has the most influence is in its consistent mix with its own applications. This permits enables simple access for students and educators to each other's work and lessens a significant number of the means already fundamental for sharing data. While different frameworks, like Schoology or Edmodo, adequately incorporate Google applications into their frameworks, they require additional means, which means additional snaps and intricacies.

Another favorable position is that items made with Google applications are intended for sharing. Sharing may more effectively happen in Google Classroom than other increasingly 'shut framework' programming frameworks.

Google Classroom may do not have a portion of the advantage's educators have come to appreciate with different frameworks like Schoology, which has reliably extended its highlights throughout the previous quite a while. Different frameworks either take into consideration instructors to make evaluations directly in the framework or effectively permit the usage of non-Google apparatuses for correspondence and assets.

Innovation in the classroom presently assumes a major job in the viability of training. Regardless of whether your students are five or fifty, it has gotten expected for instructors and mentors to use innovation so as to more readily impart course material. Numerous instructive associations offer courses that no longer need to happen in a traditional classroom. This incorporates language schools, universities and instructional class suppliers, a considerable lot of which presently offer a wide scope of sight and sound courses on the web.

Be that as it may, the decision here does not involve settling on the traditional strategy or the digital one. Schools and other preparing suppliers do not need to conclude whether to offer their seminars exclusively on the web or disconnected premise. Or maybe, numerous instructive associations are presently trying to offer courses that offer the most flawless of the two choices.

In spite of the fact that online sight and sound courses are a brilliant choice for some, many students incline toward physical classes. Numerous traditional instructive associations are currently offering virtual learning situations (VLEs) that their students can sign into, outside of fixed classroom hours, so as to benefit from the considerable upsides of virtual courses.

In addition, it is presently getting progressively easy for instructors and guides to incorporate innovation in the classroom so as to upgrade the benefits of those fixed classroom hours.

1. Consider the Flipped Classroom Model

If you have not yet heard the term' flipped classroom,' you will. This is an instructive model that is quickly spreading in popularity across different pieces of the world, including Europe, the UK and America.

The possibility of the flipped classroom model is that more ought to be done to take advantage of significant classroom time. Rather than utilizing this in-person time for an instructor to remain at the front of the room, there ought to be an approach to impart that substance to students in advance, so exercise time can be utilized for conversation, discussion, questions and guided activities.

Schools, universities and administrators, who have put resources into a conveyance framework for sight and sound courses (for e.g. a learning the board framework (LMS) or learning content administration framework [LCMS]) can utilize this to investigate a flipped classroom strategy.

Rather than giving students traditional schoolwork assignments of activities or correction identifying with the subject of the last class, take a look at giving them look into assignments to get some answers concerning the subject of the following one. This could be as straightforward as requesting that they take a look at a couple of related reports or could be giving them a couple of book sections to peruse or even a pre-recorded video talk to watch. The thought is that by doing this examination ahead of time, students will show up in class, definitely knowing a portion of the key themes of the subject, and the instructor/mentor will have the option to use this flipped classroom to invest less energy effectively gathering information and the improvement and comprehension of that lecture.

2. Take Formal Evaluations on The Web

One of the greatest timesavers that online sight and sound courses offer instructors are computerized evaluations. Many learning the board frameworks (LMS) or content administration frameworks (LCMS) offer educators the opportunity to plan and execute quality appraisal practices on the web.

In any case, obviously, there is no reason why this equivalent strategy cannot be utilized in the classroom. Why not make appraisals progressively intuitive and dynamic for students and spare the educator's time, by inviting students to sit their evaluations in class utilizing their PC or tablet?

3. Utilize A Digital Whiteboard

One of the key benefits of utilizing a virtual classroom to convey live sight and sound courses is the addition of the virtual whiteboard. This bit of tech permits instructors to share video, pictures, sound clasps, applications and more within a virtual classroom condition.

This tech is not simply accessible on the web. Actually, a digital whiteboard can be an exceptionally viable method for utilizing innovation in the classroom. Instructors can utilize it to do everything that should be possible on a virtual whiteboard. It could likewise be utilized to invite virtual visiting teachers into the classroom, utilizing video talking programming, such as Skype.

4. Run Different Activities Simultaneously

It can once in a while be hard to oversee diverse ability levels within the classroom. Innovation can help with this, as instructors can use online devices to offer various students' various activities. By utilizing sight and sound courses, teachers can set various gatherings of students up with various errands, then move around the classroom to offer them support when required.

Teaching and Learning Strategies in Virtual Education

Esteban (2009) explains that the teaching and learning strategies used in virtual education are generally classified according to cognitive activities. In accordance with this criterion, they are classified from the most basic operations to the most elaborate in association, elaboration, organization, and support. Associative strategies are the simplest, and they involve basic operations that do not in themselves promote relations between knowledge. But they can be the basis for its subsequent elaboration since they increase the probability of literally remembering the information without introducing structural changes in it. An example in a virtual classroom is the forum used in Block 0, which contains and makes known to the students all the information on the course, the resources, etc.

The elaboration strategies, according to the author in reference, constitute an intermediate step between the strictly associative ones, which do not work on the information itself, and the organizational ones, which promote new knowledge structures. In the elaboration, simpler operations can be produced, in which some relationships, generally extrinsic, are established between elements of the information that can serve as 'scaffolding' for learning, through the elaboration of meanings and other more complex things, based on the significance of the information elements. An example of this is the construction section that is placed in the academic block of the virtual classroom; there the student finds the truth via his own means and the support of his classmates; the tutor in that section does not interact.

Organizational strategies consist of establishing, in an explicit way, internal relationships between the elements that make up the learning materials and with the prior knowledge that the subject possesses. An example of its use in the virtual classroom is the exhibition section belonging to the academic block, in which all the necessary information that the student should know of, with the help of videos, files, web page links, among others, is exposed.

Finally, support strategies are those that, according to Esteban, instead of providing learning, have the mission of increasing the effectiveness of that learning by improving the conditions in which it occurs. An example is the bounce section placed in the academic block; its aim is for the apprentice to assimilate and establish relationships between what they already know and the new learnings presented, with the help and collaboration of their peers. Among the suggested activities are forums, wikis, chats, videoconferences, and blogs, through which knowledge is shared, and confrontations are generated regarding the information provided by the tutor.

These conceptions of the different strategies lead us to reflect on the 'how,' the 'what,' and the 'why' to teach in the virtual educational scenario in such a way that, in order to answer some questions. Taking into consideration the classification of the strategies of the aforementioned author, it can be deduced that there are implicit elements in each: In the organization strategies, the teacher represents the establishment of the necessary structure for the rational systematization of the content, the interaction resources, consultation spaces and the activities of interaction, through the determination of hierarchies, arrangement, correlation and grouping of activities, in order to perform and simplify the functions in virtual education.

In associative and preparation, the teacher promotes communication, which includes the time to tutor, interact and evaluate directly; This action is related to the personalization of education since students are served in the same way in which they seek to link with them. This way the methods and techniques used are understood and internalized, and the success expected in the program is obtained. process of teaching and learning. This is achieved through interaction between users and the teacher based on learning and collaborative work. The evaluation process is then clear and concrete, encourages comparison and criticality, and allows negotiation and supports recovery. From the latter, support strategies are generated in open motivation.

CHAPTER - 7

THE BEST GOOGLE CLASSROOM EXTENSION

Google Classroom's fundamental functions are strong. Take it to the subsequent degree with some accessories created simplest for instructors and students.

The fundamental capabilities of Google Drive and Google Classroom are simply the starting point for the innovative and creative programs that may be observed in the study room.

SlideShot

SlideShot is a Google Chrome alternative. It produces a screenshot each minute and will shop the photo on Google Drive. The screenshots can be automatically imported right into a presentation on Google Slides when you click Finish. The slide presentation may be found on Google Drive in the SlideShot tab. Suggestion to apply a New clear out in Drive for a short position.

How to apply it: Students can create a description of their work using this Chrome extension and Web tools. Each slide offers space for the students to feature a textual content field to demonstrate their concept and mastery. Students can pick out Attach, to feature the presentation of Google Drive Slides to their project.

Take an image of your screen (screenshot) every minute. Position on and screenshot a specific slide in a blank Google Slides Presentation This is useful in assisting college students to look again on their day jobs, and think about what they have discovered or how they have spent their time.

Group Creator

Group Creator helps you to assign college students to train at random, using the roster in your magnificence.

How to use it: Fill inside the column to your roster. Adjust the length of the group to a range of scholars in each faculty. Go to Add-ons > Team Builder > Start. Then, click on the Build Team button.

List Docs

List Docs does because it sounds like: it lists all of the documents the students send from Google Classroom. It makes a one-sheet spreadsheet containing a listing of all of the folders for your Google Classroom, and the corresponding tabs display all of the files of the scholars in each folder.

How to apply it: In the connection below, the prototype is opened. You will want to encompass the folder ID of your Google Classroom folder (which Alice tells you inside the weblog submit above). Run the Show me all of the files add-on (Great name, huh?), which has already been pre-loaded into the computer. A spreadsheet with links to all your files can be developed.

Teacher Newsletter

This one is satisfactory; however, some setup is needed first.

Teacher Newsletter helps the academics to create unique, personalized newsletters for each scholar. For each pupil, it could contain one-off gratitude, unique desires, etc. It then routinely emails those newsletters to parents.

How to do it: Basically, the use of the prototype at the connection below. Save your email to Google Docs. Attach the merge tags to the newsletter, wherein the simple details each scholar wishes to deliver in. (If the phrase 'merge tags' sounds overwhelming, do not worry ... the whole step-by-step instructions in Alice's published work will display you the way to do it.). Add each scholar's call and electronic mail with the sheet, alongside any related comments/ data to be sent to their parents. Then run the add-on and send the ones custom newsletters to parents!

Reply Maker

The Reply Maker permits you to e-mail every student with a speedy remark and without problems. With one PC, you could get to send an email to anyone.

How to use it: Open the spreadsheet inside the connection below. Copy and paste the students' names and their email addresses. Kind individual remarks for every pupil. You also can add a worldwide message, a remark that is going to everybody and chooses not to ship e-mails to unique students. Tap the Return Emails button, and you are done!

Pull the Paragraph

You can read anything on one web page, type Enter, and send it to the students.

How to do this: Open your Google Drive to a Student Work tab (if you are familiar with the use of Google Classroom, it is going to be within the Classroom folder). Removing the paragraph in the desk will take the writing of all the college students. You will want to enlarge the columns, and use word wrap to peer greater. Read scholar, take a look at it, and type comments to respond to them within the remark section. Pull the paragraph can then apply some feedback to the documents of the scholars and will also provide them with an e-mail telling them that there may be input to see.

RosterTab

For each student, create a spreadsheet with a tab, allowing every scholar to paintings their virtual area within a whole class report. RosterTab will create all those tabs for you immediately.

How to do this: Copy and paste (or kind in) the names of all the students. Go to Add-ons > RosterTab2 > Start and generate every pupil's tabs. It is proper to have college students do a little simple study that is compiled within the same report so that you do not have to open several files to score.

RubricTab

TemplateTab sets off yet every other one. RubricTab copies, on this edition, a rubric for each pupil tab you create. You can supply a grade and provide remarks approximately any pupil's rubric. When you are finished, you can get replica/paste and electronic mail a link to every scholar's page.

How to Use It

- Leave a new call for the recipient. This is the rubric structure.

- Enter the name of the task into mobile F1. For each scholar named with the project name, the venture name is used to assemble spreadsheets.

- Place the range of points in cell D3 in which possible.

- Leave open feedback. This is the rubric structure.

- Row 8 sets a percentage fee for weights in each group. When rubric rankings that a rubric score does not convert to a percentage, note. In different words, a score of not 50% is two out of four. You can alternate the possibilities set through default.

- Each rubric criterion is weighed equally by using default settings. Delete those chances via default and update them with the values you want.

- Replace the text of the criterion along with your rubric criterion.

- Replace the causes of the default parameters with your own definition. Note that every cell has a default wording formula. A single click on at the cell to trade the default text and begin typing your definition.

- Further parameters can be applied in column C. Start typing in C13 and so forth your fifth criterion.

In Google Drive, a folder of the same name is created for each assignment you make in Google Classroom. Drill down from Google Drive's Classroom tab to the undertaking tab magnificence folder. You can without difficulty get the right of entry to that in Google Classroom by using clicking from the mission at the Folder tab.

CHAPTER - 8

TOP 5 HIDDEN FEATURES OF GOOGLE CLASSROOM

Google Classroom Hidden Features

Google Classroom provides a productive workflow for teachers and students by arranging courses and class contents in an easy-to-navigate online environment, thanks to its capabilities to seamlessly incorporate G Suite tools such as Google Documents, Google Slides, Google Papers, Gmail and Google Calendars. Although Google Classroom provides many great opportunities, three can save teachers and students a lot of time and improve workflow capacity. So, let us use these exciting apps!

1. The Assignment Calendar

Google Classroom Assignment Calendar automatically generates an assignment calendar to better coordinate students and teachers. Whenever a teacher inside the Google Classroom creates a job or query and adds a due date, the task will automatically be on the class calendar inside Google Classroom.

Find the three-lined button in the top left corner of the screen for this calendar and click Date. Teachers and students can see the work assigned to the class on this computer.

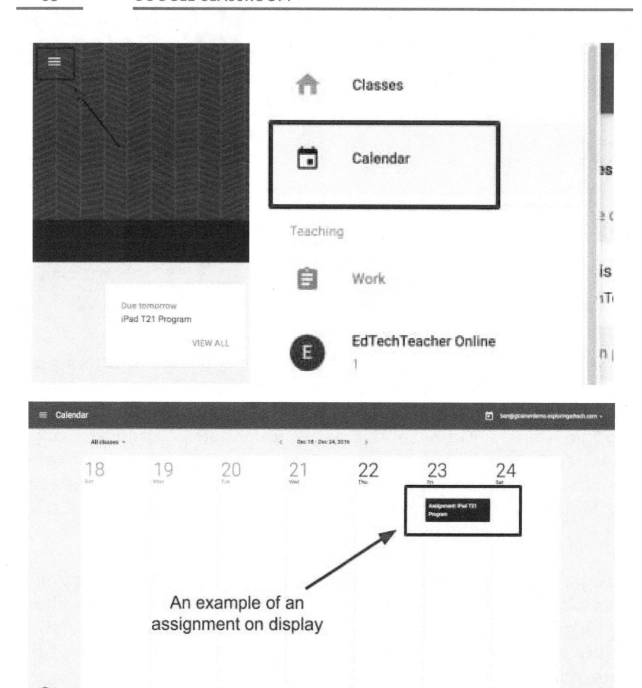

An example of an
assignment on display

Teachers will also note that their G Suite schedule now contains a
new calendar. Not only can teachers assign activities to this schedule
via the classroom, but they can also access it directly through the
G Suite Calendar, to assign events for a class not bound to the due

date. Examples of teachers who use this calendar feature include organizing field trips, providing extra tutoring time, and scheduling a post-school meeting. To make the calendar more available, make it public in the settings of the calendar, and then share the URL link with the parents.

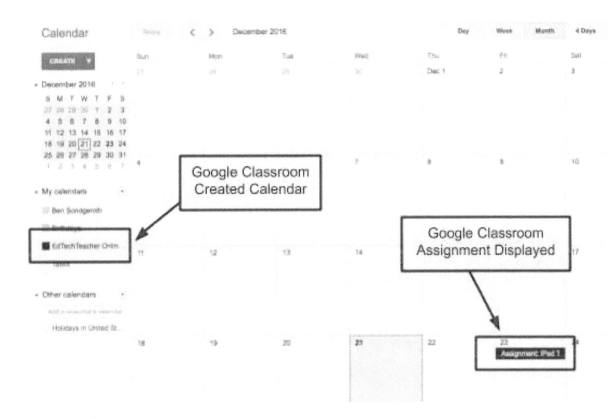

2. The Work Area

Teachers and students may also take advantage of the Google Classroom's workspace to gather all outstanding jobs in one place. The work area may also serve as a default task list and allow teachers and students to define and control their workflow efficiently.

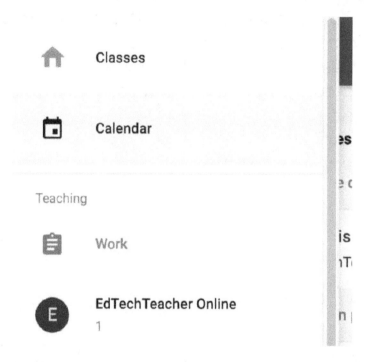

3. Organize a Class Stream with Topics

A new function inside Google Classroom enables teachers to organize the posts that they attach to the 'Path' classroom, and now teachers can allocate a subject to the announcement, assignment, or query, which can be organized efficiently for each post.

When a new topic is created, the problem will be displayed on the left side of the classroom stream, and all the posts related to that topic will appear when an item is selected. The themes now enable teachers to organize all material in their course. A history teacher may, for instance, create a subject for each study unit such as 'Ancient Rome.' A math teacher can choose to create a topic for each study unit or chapter.

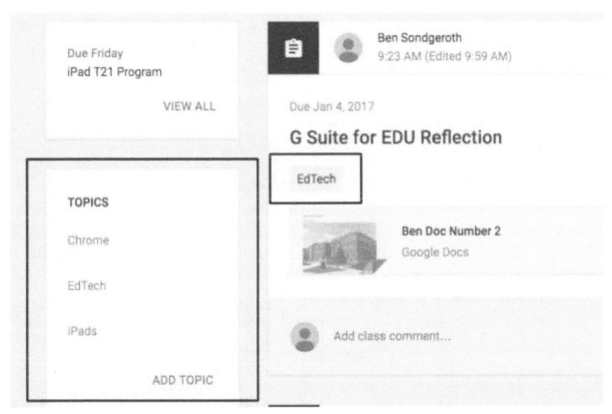

4. Share to Classroom Extension

For teachers in school classrooms using Chromebooks or tablets, Chrome Extension Sharing helps teachers to view and sharing student work and screens quickly. The Share to Classroom extension allows students to access a website on the machine of the instructor. Students first click on the expansion and then select

Move to Instructor. When done, the instructor will receive a pop-up message on their computer, that they must approve it before the student's page is shown.

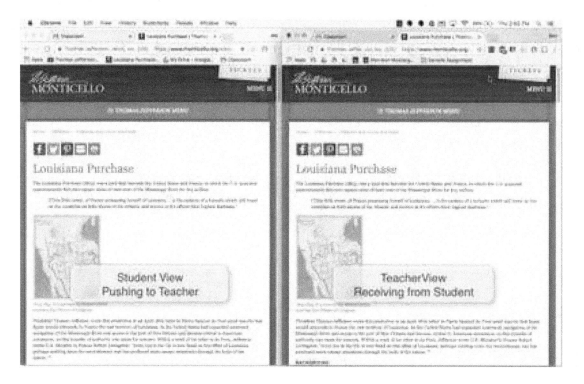

Through following the same steps, a teacher will push a website in real-time to the devices of his students!

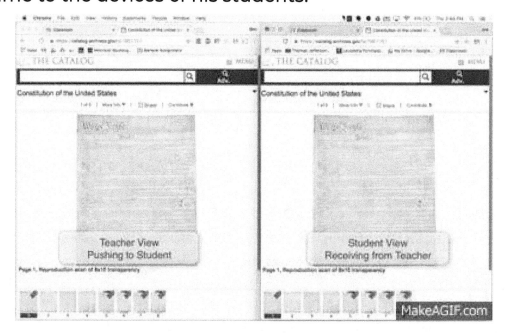

Teachers can also create Google Classroom material directly from the extension. When a professor discovers a website he or she needs to add as part of a mission, query, or announcement in Google Classroom, he or she may use the extension to build any of those choices.

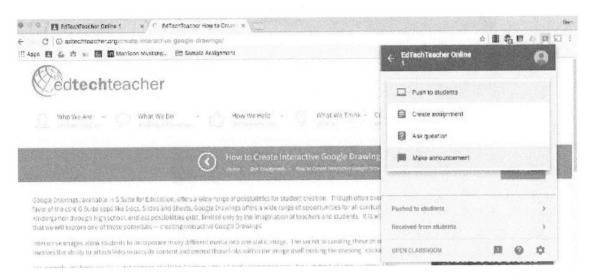

With the Share to Classroom extension, teachers and students now can quickly and efficiently share new insights and stories.

5. Wrapping It Up

On the other hand, Google Classroom is well known for organizing their students' research on Google Drive, making copies of Google Docs and the organization of digital materials. These three under-used features of Google Classroom will help you and your students make their use of classroom technology much more productive!

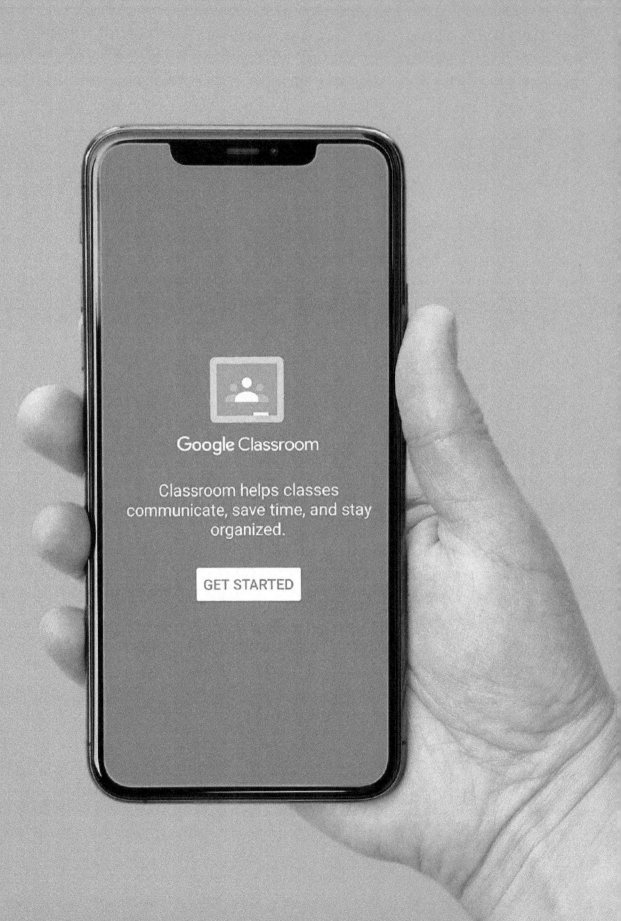

CHAPTER - 9

TOP USEFUL APPS FOR GOOGLE CLASSROOM

While Google Classroom can be used by anyone wanting to teach and learn, mostly, it is built for schools, so having an ID for the G Suite and accessing the site via the ID helps keep things organized in the online sphere for administration purposes in a school. It ensures that you do not mix your private/personal documents and information into your Google Drive or Gmail account, connected to your Suite.

Here they are!

1. TESTeach

CREATE	ENGAGE	ASSESS
Save time by collecting all digital content in one place	Achieve learning goals with fun, interactive lessons	Monitor student understanding with quizzes and discussions

TESTeach is one of those must-have applications to integrate with your Google Classroom, as it has plenty of lessons, presentations, and projects. You can create interactive content using TESTeach and use it on your Google Classroom.

2. CLASS CRAFT

3. Discovery Education

Techbook™ Digital Textbooks

Lead with content. Engage with digital. That's the hallmark of Discovery Education Techbook. Standards-based with content that is relevant and dynamic. Techbook helps teachers differentiate and improve achievement with easy-to-use tools and resources.

Discovery Education is another source of well-curated information loaded into digital textbooks, digital media, and Virtual Field Trips, that feature content that is relevant and dynamic. They also have easy-to-use tools and resources that enable teachers to include them in their differentiated learning modules, to improve their student's achievements.

4. CK12

You can download this app either in student mode or teacher mode. If you plan on creating a differentiated assignment, then this website is your holy grail, because it is filled with a library of online textbooks, flashcards, exercise videos, and all of it is for free!

5. GEOGEBRA

GeoGebra Math Calculators with Graphing, Geometry, 3D, Spreadsheet, CAS and more!

Geometry Calculator   Graphing Calculator   3D Calculator

Materials   GeoGebra Graphing Calculator for Android   Downloads

Geogebra is an excellent application for both educators and students alike. It includes a graphing calculator, 3D Calendar, and geometry calculator that can be used to produced geometry, calculus, statistics, and 3D math and functions.

6. Alma

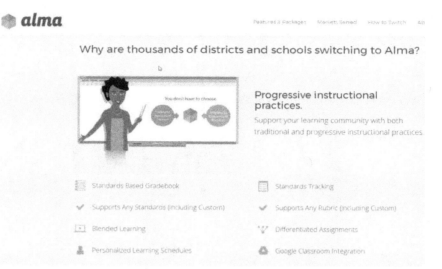

Alma is a refreshing and sleek software designed to help schools and teachers improve their school management, learning management systems, and student information systems. Its interface is user-friendly, and it has operations with grading, standards tracking, and supports any kind of rubric.

7. BUNCEE

Discover   Resources   For Schools   buncee⬤

The Tool that Fosters Creativity

Easy to use for students of all ages, Buncee encourages them to reach their full potential. Create a fun learning environment in the classroom while engaging students both at home and at school.

Visualize

Easily bring your critical thinking and creativity to life.

Encourage your student's creativity through Buncee, a presentation tool that is highly interactive and loaded with an extensive list of visualization components. Buncee allows students as well as educators to create highly visual and interactive presentation stickers, animation, and built-in templates. Buncee is currently used in over 127 countries.

8. Google Cultural Institute

The Google Cultural Institute features an online collection of art, exhibits, and archives sourced from around the world. Need to link an assignment with content? Look it up on Google Cultural Institute. You can find an extensive list of topics and articles categorized under experiments, historical events, movements as well as artists curated from museums and archives worldwide.

9. Curiosity

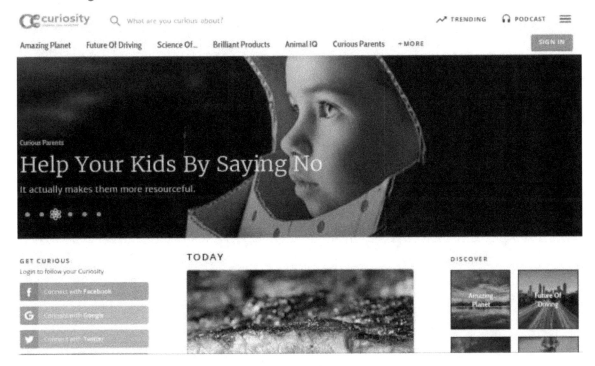

This application curates and creates content for learners all around the world. Editors look for content and present it in the best way possible. Curiosity can be accessed through the website or their app.

10. DUOLINGO

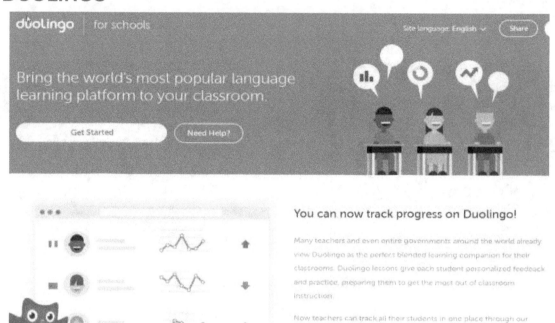

Duolingo is, by far, the world's most popular language website.

11. EDPUZZLE

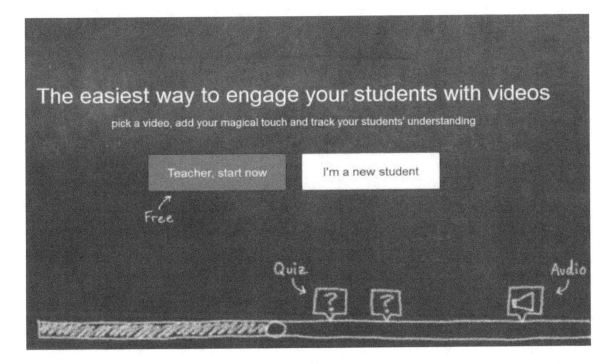

To be used by both educators as well as learners, Edpuzzle allows you to create your videos and include interactive lessons, voice over, audio, and many more function, to turn any video into an experience. What is more, teachers can also track if a student watches the videos, the answers they give, and how many times they view a video.

12. Flat

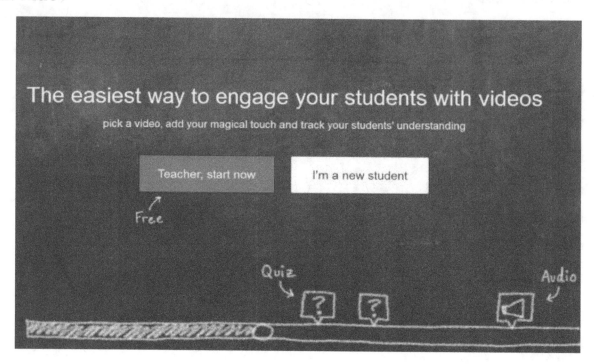

You can integrate Google Classroom with Flat Education and synchronize existing rosters in your Classroom, as well as design new activities that students can access via class.

13. LISTENWISE

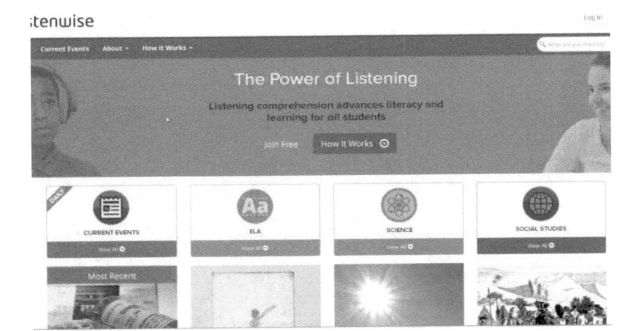

This listening skills platform harnesses the power of listening to empower learning and literacy for students. This site features podcasts and public radio content.

14. LUCIDPRESS

**QUICKLY CREATE AND SHARE
STUNNING VISUAL CONTENT**

Encourage your students to create visually stunning materials for their assignments using Lucidpress. From newsletters to brochures, digital magazines to online flyers, Lucipress incorporates an intuitive interface of drag-and-drop, that is easy for beginners and also for experienced designers.

15. NEARPOD

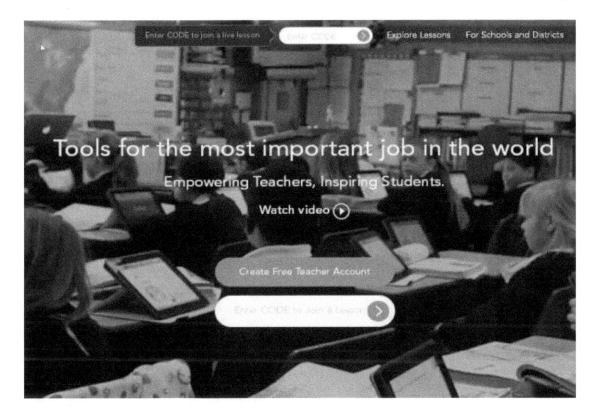

Create intuitive lessons with Nearpod, whether in JPEG or PDF files, and upload them to your Google Classroom. Nearpod enables teachers to create mobile presentations and share and control the display in real-time.

16. NEWSELA

With NEWSELA, you can integrate articles into your assignments with embedded assessments. Start a dialogue, customize prompts, and facilitate close reading with this app.

17. PBS Learning Media

The PBS Learning Media is a standards-aligned digital resource that gives educators and students access to digital resources, for both student and professional development.

18. QUIZZEZ

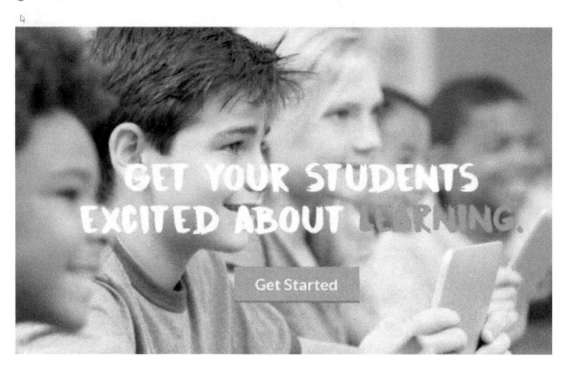

With built-in avatars, music, memes, leaderboards, and themes, Quizzez enables a teacher to easily create engaging quizzes that can be uploaded to Google Classroom. Teachers can also obtain student-level data while the exams are being played.

19. RMBOOKS

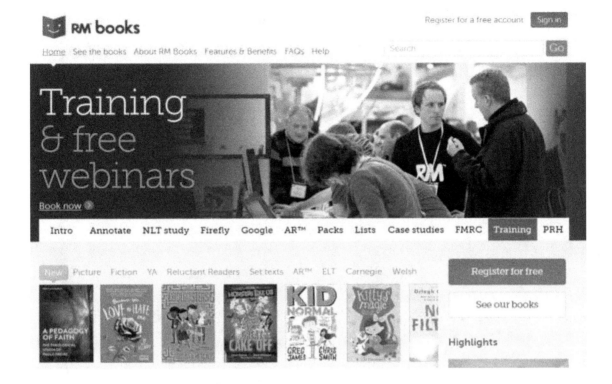

If you conduct reading and writing classes, then this add-on is for you. RM Books is an e-book solution designed specifically for schools. It is a service that requires no upfront payment. Students can access digital textbooks, classic literature, and new releases from a wide array of genres.

20. Science Buddies

Get connected to thousands of resources for your student's science project, from convenient kits to summer science camps, science blogs, and many more.

21. TEXTHELP

It is another excellent tool for reading and writing classes. Texthelp can be used in Google Classroom as a support tool for languages, reading, comprehension, and writing.

22. VERSAL

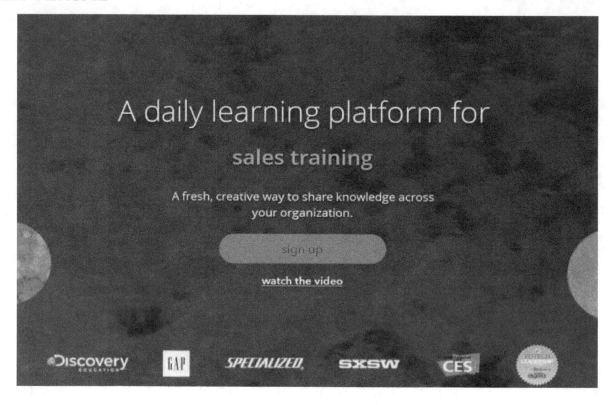

If you are using Google Classroom for professional development, then this website is for you. Versal is a platform for everyday learning with its content geared to helping companies create a vibrant culture of collaborative knowledge sharing.

23. WEVIDEO

WeVideo is the online video editor that makes it easy to capture, create, view and share your movies at up to 4K resolution for stunning playback anywhere.

It can be used for higher education, life, school, students, and teachers. Wevideo takes video sharing to a new level, by empowering people to create story-telling video formats and share their stories with powerful video editing features.

CHAPTER - 10

DOCS, SHEET, AND SLIDES

Google Drive

This has cloud storage of about 15GB that allows users to store all data without a cost, but you should have an internet connection to access them. This is a fantastic tool that stores diverse types of files, including PDF files, audio, images, videos, documents, etc.; you simply need to upload the data, and then it is safe and secure.

Another thing you need to know about Google Drive is the ability to link up with others, sharing files, sharing them with your students to download, view, and create files to a central folder. You can share anything with other teachers as well as students. This is the best form of file organization for pupils, their parents, or even your colleagues to access.

Just when you think that you always have to be online to view files or data, boom! You can access your files offline by setting your Google Drive offline. Nice right? Yes, I know.

Google Docs

This is different from Google Drive, as some people know. This is the same with Microsoft Word, except that it is free and online, you must have an internet connection to access it. The bright side of this tool is its ability for students to do a collaborative assignment without the regular transferring of documents. They can all access the same report online and its in-built chatting module. Also, it takes us to the paperless age, where we do not have to write on papers.

Google Slides

Google Classroom combined with other Google products, such as Google Slides, can deliver powerful interactive user experiences and deliver engaging and valuable content. Teachers looking to create engaging experiences in Google Classroom can use Google Slides and other tools in the Google Suite of products, to create unique experiences.

Discussed below are some exciting ways that you can use Google Classroom and Google Slides to create an engaging learning experience for your students:

Create eBooks via PDF

PDF files are so versatile, and you can open them in any kind of device. Want to distribute information only for read-only purposes? Create a PDF! You can use Google Docs or even Google Slides for this purpose, and then save it as a PDF document before sending it out to your classroom.

Create A Slide Deck Book

Make your textbooks paperless too, not just assignments. Teachers can derive engaging and interactive content from the web, include it in the slide deck books, upload it to the Google Classroom, and allow your students to access them. Make sure to keep it as read-only.

Play Jeopardy

This method has been used in plenty of Google Classrooms, and the idea was created by Eric Curts, who is a Google Certified Innovator. This template can be copied into your own Google Drive so you can customize your question and answers. Scores can be kept on another slide that only you can control.

Create Game-Show Style Review Games

Another creative teacher came up with a Google Slide of 'Who Wants to Be a Millionaire?' The template allows you to add in your questions and get students to enter the answers in the text box. Again, you keep the score!

Use Animation

Did you know you can create animations in your Google Slide and share them in your Classroom? This tutorial shows you how. You can also encourage your students to create an animation to explain their assignments. This is making them push boundaries and think out of the box.

Create Stories and Adventures

Use Google Slides and upload them to Google Classroom to tell a story. Turn a question into a story and teach your students to create an adventure to describe their decision of the outcome of the character in their story. The stories can be a certain path that the students have chosen for the character of a story that explains the process of finding a solution.

Using Flash Cards

Flashcards are great ways to increase the ability to understand a subject or topic. Do you want to create an interactive session on Google Classroom using flashcards? You can start by utilizing Google Sheets, which gives you a graphic display of words and questions. To reveal the answers, all you need to do is click. Compared to paper flashcards, these digital flashcards allow you to easily change the questions, colors as well as the answers of the cards, depending on what you are teaching the class. Digital flashcards are also an interactive presentation method that is guaranteed to engage your Classroom, and bring about a new way of teaching using Google Classroom's digital space. Make vocabulary lessons, geography lessons, and even history lessons fun and entertaining, with digital flashcards.

Host an Online Viewing Party

Get your students to connect to the Classroom at a pre-determined date and time, when there is a noteworthy performance, play, or even a movie, that is related to the subjects you are teaching in your class. Let them view the video together, and also interact with them by adding questions to your Google Classroom and allowing your students to reply to you in real-time. This way, you can assess them on their reflections, level of understanding, and their observations. You can also give your interpretation of the scene and explain it again to students who do not quite understand.

Google Sheets

It is a cloud-based software that is similar to Microsoft Excel. You do not even need to learn to use it, as it is been created to mirror Excel for easier adoption.

Strengths

- Automatic saving to Drive as you work.

- Allows real-time collaboration and tracking of changes.

- You can send emails as you comment on individual or groups of cells.

Weaknesses

- Cells are not as intuitive compared to Excel cells. Formulas do not automatically correct themselves if you move cells around.

- The formatting options, in terms of the appearance of your spreadsheets, are limited.

- The default size of your sheet is smaller than Excel and is tedious to enlarge.

CHAPTER - 11

HOW TO CREATE AND ORGANIZE TOPICS IN CLASSWORK PAGE

Topics, a feature inside Google Classroom allows teachers to organize the posts they add to the classroom Stream.

When a different topic is formed, it will display all posts on the left side of the Classroom Stream that has been assigned to that subject, which will appear if a subject is chosen. The 'Topics' feature now allows teachers to organize all content within their course. For instance, a history teacher might create a topic for each study unit, such as 'Ancient Rome.' For each unit or chapter they study, a math teacher may choose to create a topic.

A recent update to Google Classroom is its ability to arrange topic-by-theme assignments. This is beneficial for you, since it helps you to have group assignments together in the Classwork tab by unit or form. Students and teachers will consider the task they are searching for more efficiently. Follow the instructions below to build Topics.

1. Navigate to Level.

2. Tap the tab Classwork.

3. Click on the Create button.

4. Select Subject.

5. Name your subject and click Add.

You may add new assignments to a subject from the development screen for the assignment. Simply select the drop-down box next to Topic before allocating it. If you have already created assignments that need to be moved to a Topic, follow these steps:

1. Tap the tab Classwork.

2. Swipe over the task with your mouse.

3. Click on the three-dotted button.

4. Pick Edit

5. Search the drop-down box next to Topic.

6. Click the drop-down button and select the topic you wish to move to.

Topics are probably the easiest way to make sure that the content that you post on the Google Classroom does not get out of hand, and it is easily accessible by you and your students. To use Topics to organize your Google classroom, go to Classwork, click Create, and click on the topic.

Before you create any topics, think about how you would like to compartmentalize everything that you have posted on your Google Classroom. You might have a bunch of assignments, questions, a bunch of materials, and so forth. Think about what are the topics that all your posts can fall into. Tutors normally compartmentalize their content by either units or types of posts.

So, let me demonstrate first, how can we categorize our post by units. So, to do that, we are going to create three units that I am teaching this semester. We are going to create unit one, create another unit, Unit 2, and Unit 3. You might have noticed that once I have created those units, they appear on the left of my screen as a table of contents. This is because I have some posts that have been generated before I can now try and sort them out. So, I know that Assignment 1 belongs to Unit 1. What I will do I will simply take it and drag it to unit one. Immediately, assignment one will disappear from my posts he up top and will show up under unit one. I will do the same for other posts. My first quiz assignment belongs to Unit 3. My question about creativity belongs to Unit 2. My essay prompts belong to Unit 3, and my Assignment 2 belongs to Unit 2. I think we have started to see how our Google Classroom can look much more organized.

When we start using topics, there are a couple of things you can do when it comes to editing the topics. The first thing is to rename them. Once you have set up a name, you can rename it later on, move them up and down, or drag them from the old topics view. One important thing to remember is that when you delete a topic, the posts that belong to this topic will not be deleted. What I have done right now I have deleted Unit 3, which had essay prompts and my first quiz assignment, but they are, they have just been moved up to an unassigned topic. So, this is one way to organize all of your content organizing by units.

What you can also do is organize all your content according to the type of the post Google Classroom allows you to create four different types of assignment quiz, assignment questions and materials; and this could be your topics. So, why do not we go ahead and try and organize in this way, our first topic is going to be an assignment. Our second topic is going to be a quiz assignment. Our third topic is going to be a question. And finally, our fourth topic is going to be a material assignment. We will go on to the assignment material, we will go on to the material, and so forth. There is one more thing I need to point out, which is that you can assign your posts to topics, while you are creating them to do that, and while you are creating. Let us say here that you can select which topic this particular post will be assigned to. This is a question I posed. So, this will be assigned to a question once I post this question, it will automatically go on to the question topic. These are just two ways to categorize your posts. You can come up with your own method, but this is what I personally do either organizing by units or types of assignments.

HOW TO CREATE AND ORGANIZE TOPICS IN CLASSWORK PAGE

Teaching Math

If you are thinking about how else you can expand the experience of learning math or using Classroom in your math classes, here are some creative ways to build on.

The Problem of the Week (POW)

POWs can be anything that you feel need more attention. It can either be a problem you have identified or a problem that your students can identify. You can create games that can help students learn about the problem differently, and participating students can submit their work directly to Google Classroom.

NUMBER LINES

1. Make each line add up to 16.

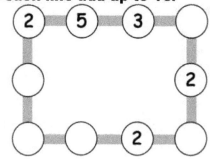

2. Make each line add up to 20.

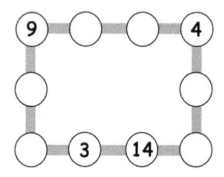

1. Link Interactive Simulations

There are several websites dedicated to providing helpful math simulations. Sites like Explore Learning have thousands of math simulations and math variations that students can look up, to solve mathematical problems. You can link these URLs in your classroom either as part of an assignment or through an announcement.

2. Link to Playsheets

Playsheets fall between gamification and GBL. Teachers can link up relevant Playsheets and give these assignments to the students. These playsheets give immediate feedback to students, and it is an excellent learning and motivational tool that tells the students that they are on the right track.

3. Use Google Draw

Google Draw is another creative tool that allows students and teachers to create virtual manipulations such as charts, algebra tiles, and so on. Draw images that make it easy for students to identify with Math. This can be used to create differentiated assignments targeting students with different learning levels.

4. Use digital tools

Digital tools such as Desmos, Geogebra, and Daum Equation Editor can also be used to solve various Math problems. These tools can be used from Google Drive and integrated with other Google documents. Once done, students can submit their solved problems to Google Classroom.

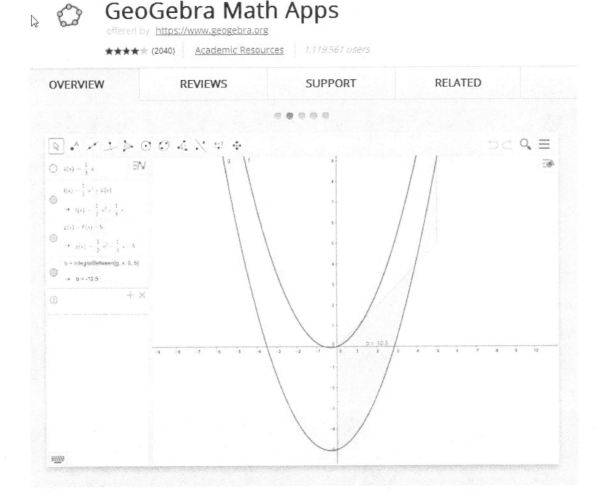

Teach Programming

Google Apps Script

Get students to use programs such as Scratch or Google Apps Script, that can enable them to exhibit their understanding of mathematical concepts.

Teaching Science

1. Hangout with Experts

Get experts you are connected to in real life to talk about their experiences working in a science-related field, to help students with their science-related subjects. You can use Google Hangouts to send questions the class has and link it to your Google Classroom. This enables the students to access the Hangout, and participate in the questioning, or even watch the interview after the session is done. The Hangout session can be archived for viewing later.

2. Collecting Evidence

Have your students submit evidence of science experiments by sending in photos or videos of their science projects and uploading it to Google Classroom.

3. Give Real Life Examples

Tailor-make your science projects and assignments, so that it gets students to go outside and get real-life samples which they can record on their mobile devices. They can take these images and submit it immediately to the Google Classroom. Make it interesting, students that submit their answers faster get extra points!

4. Crowdsourcing Information

Get students into the whole activity of crowdsourcing. Create a Google Spreadsheet with a specific topic and specify what information they need, and what goals the project needs to accomplish. Upload the document to Google Classroom, and get students to find and contribute information.

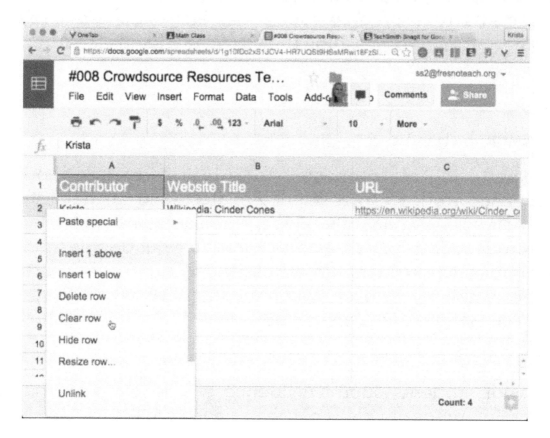

Teaching Writing & Reading

1. Provide Templates

Allow students to access writing templates on Google Classroom for things such as formal letters, informal letters, report writing, assignment templates, resumes, and cover letter formats.

2. Reading Records

Establish a weekly reading record on Google Classroom where they can record information on the times that they have read during the week. So instead of writing it down on a reading diary, allow them to update a form on Google Classroom by entering the necessary data. This allows them to immediately add in the information of the books, that they have read while it is still fresh in their minds.

Class Reading Record

Tom Barrett
ICT in my Classroom - http://tbarrett.edublogs.org

Name

Date

Book Title

Page Numbers

Comments
What did you enjoy? Did you struggle with any words? What help did you get?

I read with...

Submit

3. Collaborate on Writing Projects

Get your students to collaborate on writing projects via group assignments. These projects can be anything from preparing newspaper articles, journals, e-portfolios, and so on.

Teaching Physical Education

Did not think PE could be done via Google Classroom? Given below are some ideas.

1. Post Fitness Videos

Post fitness videos to help your students understand how to perform a workout. Send out videos to any psychical activity that you want students to conduct in their next PE session, or you can also just post a video after classes, so students can practice the exercise in their own time and work on their form.

2. Get Students to Post Videos Of Their Daily Workout

Have your students post videos in the public feed on your Google Classroom with a hashtag such as #midweekfitspo. Encourage students to work out and post their videos each week.

3. Link to Safety Videos

Post safety videos for your PE activities, so your students know what kind of skills they need to follow to exercise safely.

4. Post Resources for Activities

PE teachers can also post useful resources for games and activities ahead of time, such as rules and methods of playing before the student's next PE session. It would help the students prepare and know what to expect for their next class.

5. Create a Fitness Tracker

Assign students to a Fitness Tracker spreadsheet and make a copy for each student. Assign a due date for the end of the semester for their physical education class. You can monitor each student's progress by checking out the assignment folder in the Google Classroom.

Use the spreadsheet to get your students to track their progress. Whenever students update their results, the spreadsheet automatically updates to dynamic charts, so students can see their progress visually over the entire semester.

You can either pair students up to work in partners or individually. Get the students to take photos of each other's forms when practicing certain tasks, so that you can evaluate their form and correct it by way of giving them feedback via Classroom or during PE classes. A rubric would be helpful here too, so that students can self-evaluate their own workouts and make corrections where necessary.

Other Teaching Methods to Use

1. Attach Patterns and Structures

Upload patterns and structures that students can identify and explain. Students can also collaborate with other students to identify patterns and structures, to come up with solutions.

2. Use Geometric Concepts

Use Google Drawings or Slides to insert drawings of geometric figures for Math, Science, and even for Art.

3. Collaborate Online with Other Teachers

If you know other teachers have modules or projects which would come in handy with your class, collaborate and enable your students to join in as well. Different teachers allow for different resources, and the teaching load can also be distributed.

4. Peer Tutoring

Senior students can also be allowed to access your Google Classroom at an agreed time on a weekly basis to tutor and give support to junior students or to students in differentiated assignments.

5. Celebrate Success

Google Classroom also enables the teacher to encourage students through comments whenever they submit an assignment because feedback can be given immediately, either privately or publicly.

6. Digital Quizzes

Quizzes can be used for various subjects on Google Classroom. Get your students to submit their answers quickly for extra points.

7. Share Presentations

Share presentations and slides with your students to help them with whatever assignments you have given them.

CHAPTER - 13

TIPS AND TRICKS TO GET THE MOST OUT OF GOOGLE CLASSROOM

Both teachers and students can benefit from Google Classroom. It is an easy platform that brings together some best apps that Google has to offer, to help teachers get the most out of their lectures, and students to learn in new and exciting ways. Here we will look at some of the tips and tricks that both students and teachers can try to get the most out of the Google Classroom platform.

Tips for Teachers

Tip 1: Learn All the Ways to Give Feedback

Your students are going to thrive with as much feedback as you can provide them, and Classroom offers you many options for this. You can leave comments on assignments that student's hand in, on the file that is submitted, through email, and so much more. Consider the best places to leave feedback, and let your students know, so they can be on the lookout for ways to improve.

Some ways that you can utilize comments include:

- Class comments: You can do this by starting a common for the whole class outside the assignment or in the announcement. This is going to be a comment that the whole class is going to see, so do not use it if you just want to talk to the individual student. It is a good option to use if you want to answer a question that a lot of people have.

- Private comments: You can do this by going into the file of an individual student. You will be able to see the submissions this student has made, and you can click on the comment bar near the bottom. When you add a comment, the student will be the only one who can see it.

- Comments to media: You can do this by clicking on the file that the student submitted to you. Highlight the area and then comment on that particular part of the project. This can help you to show an example of the student or explain your thoughts on how something needs to be changed.

Tip 2: Use the Description Feature

When creating an assignment, make sure to add a nice long description. This is where you explain what the assignment is all about, how to complete it, and when the assignment is due. Often students are juggling many classes all at once and by the time they get to the assignment, they have forgotten all the instructions you gave them in class. Maybe if a student missed class that day, the description can help them understand what they missed. A good description can help to limit emails with questions and can help students get started on the assignment without confusion.

Tip 3: Use Flubaroo

Grading can take up a lot of your time, especially when dealing with many students and multiple classes. You want to provide your students with accurate feedback as quickly as possible, but traditional teaching can make this impossible. Add-ons like Flubaroo can make this easier. When creating a quiz or test, you can use Flubaroo, so that when a student submits their answers, the application will check them and provide a score right away. The student can see how well they did on the quiz, and where they may need to make some changes.

This kind of add-on is best for things such as multiple-choice assignments and tests. It allows the student to see what they understand right away, without having to wait for the teacher to correct everything. You are able to go back and change the grade on a particular assignment if the add-on grades incorrectly, or if you want to add bonus points, or for some other reason.

If you are creating assignments like discussion posts, opinions, projects, and essays, Flubaroo is not the best option for you. This application is not going to understand how to grade these projects, and since each one is more creative and does not necessarily have a right or wrong answer, it is important for the teacher to go in and grade. There are many places where you can provide feedback, even at various points of the project, to help the student make changes before the final grade.

Tip 4: Reuse Some of Your Old Posts

At times, you may have an assignment, question, or announcement that is similar to something you have posted before. For example, if you have a weekly reading or discussion assignment that is pretty much the same every week, you will be able to use the Reuse option in the Classroom. To do this, just click on the + button on the right of the screen. You will then be able to select Reuse post. Pick from a list of options that you already used for the class. If there are any modifications, such as a different due date, you can make those before posting again. When reusing the post, you have the option to create new copies of the attachments that were used in the original post.

Tip 5: Share Your Links and Resources

There may be times that you find an interesting document, video, or other media that you would like your students to see. Or they may need resources for an upcoming project, and you want to make it easier for them to find. In this case, you should use the announcement feature. This allows all the important documents to be listed right at the top of the classroom, rather than potentially getting lost further down in assignments.

This is a great tip to use for items of interest that you would like to share with your students or for documents and files that they will need right away. If you have a resource that the students will need throughout the year, you should place it into the About tab, to prevent it getting lost as the year goes on.

Tips for Students

Tip 1: Pick One Email for All of Your Classes

Consider having a dedicated email for all of your classes. You do not need to separate it and have an email for each of your classes but create a new email that will only accept information from all classes using Google Classroom. Whenever a teacher announces they use this platform, you will use this email. This helps you to keep all of your classes in one place. It can prevent you from missing out on your announcements and assignments because they got lost in all your personal emails.

Tip 2: Check Your Classes Daily

As the year goes on, your teacher will probably get into a routine of when they make posts, and you can check the class at that time. But it is still a good idea to stay on top of a class and check it each day. You never know when you may forget about an assignment that is almost due, or when the teacher will add an extra announcement for the whole class. If you only check your classes on occasion, you could miss out on a lot of important information along the way. Check-in daily to stay up to date and to get everything in on time.

Tip 3: Look at The Calendar

One of the first places you should go when opening up to a class is the Calendar. This is going to list everything important that is coming your way in the next few months (updated as the teacher adds new announcements and assignments), so you can plan out your time. For some students, it is easier to get a grasp on the work when it is in table form, rather than just looking at a date in the announcements. Use this as a planning tool and check it often to see if there is anything new to add to your schedule.

Tip 4: Ask Questions for Clarification

Classroom makes it easier for students to ask the questions they need before starting an assignment. In some classrooms, it can be hard to find time to ask a question. When twenty or more students are asking questions at the same time, or the teacher runs out of time and barely gets the assignment out before the next bell, there are many students who may leave the classroom without any clue how to begin on an assignment.

With Classroom, the students can ask any questions they have when it is convenient. If they have a question about an assignment, they can comment on the assignment or send an email. If they have a question about some feedback that is left for a test, discussion, or essay, they can ask it right in the Assignment. Classroom has opened up many options for talking to your teacher and getting your questions answered, so do not be shy and sit in the dark when you need clarification.

Tip 5: Learn About All the Features of Google

Google has many great features that both students and teachers can take advantage of. Many people do not realize all the different apps that are available on Google, and since these apps can be used together with Classroom and are free, it is important to take advantage of as many as possible. Some of the best Google products that can help with learning include:

- Gmail: Gmail makes it easier for students and teachers to communicate about the class without sharing the information with other students.

- Calendar: Students will be able to see at a glance when important assignments, tests, and other information occurs in their class.

- Drive: Drive is a great place to put all assignments, questions, and other documents that are needed to keep up in class. Teachers can place learning materials and assignments inside for the student to see and students can submit their assignments all in one place.

- YouTube: Students are used to spending time on YouTube, and teachers can use this to their advantage to find educational videos for their class. Students can either look at links that the teacher provides or search for their videos.

- Docs: This program works similarly to Microsoft Word, but since it is free, it can be nice for those students who do not already have Word at home. Students can write, edit, and make changes just like on regular documents and then submit them back to the teacher.

- Google Earth/Maps: Explore the world around us with these two great features. Google Earth lets students learn more about the world, by allowing them to look up different areas and see them from an actual satellite. Google Maps can help with Geography around the world, and students can even create their Maps with this program.

These are just a few of the different apps available with Google that can make a difference in the way that students learn. While not all of them will apply to every class, a good understanding of each can help the teacher pick the right one for their class and can help the student learn as much as possible.

CHAPTER - 14

FREQUENTLY ASKED QUESTIONS

Is Google Classroom Accessible to Users With Disabilities?

Yes, the Classroom is committed to improving accessibility for the users, which includes those with disabilities.

What Does Google Classroom Cost?

The Classroom is free for all users.

Who Is Eligible for Google Classroom?

The Classroom is available to individuals over 13 years old, with personal Google Accounts. The ages may vary from country to country. It is also available to schools through G Suite for Education, and to organizations that use G Suite for non-profits.

Is There a Google Classroom Application For My Tablet Or Phone?

Yes. The Google Classroom application is available for iOS, Chrome, Apple and Android devices.

How Is Google Classroom Different from Using A Personal Account To A School Account?

Google Classroom is commonly the same for all users. Nevertheless, since the users who use school accounts can access the G Suite for Education, they have additional features like full administration of user accounts and email summaries of students' work for guardians.

The users of G Suite for nonprofits receive the same features as that of the users of G Suite for Education.

Will I Be Able to Use Google Classroom If Gmail Is Disabled On My G Suite For Education Domain?

Yes, there is no need to enable your Gmail in order to use the Classroom. But if your administrator has not enabled Gmail, students and teachers will not receive email notifications. One note to keep in mind is that if you have your own mail server set up and you receive Drive notifications, you will also receive notifications from Google Classroom.

If the School Does Not Use G Suite For Education, Can I Use Google Classroom With My Students With Personal Accounts?

No, to be able to use Google Classroom with students in a school, the school has to sign up for a free account in G Suite for Education. Then, the schools would be able to decide which Google services can be used by teachers and students. In addition, through the G Suite for Education, students and teachers will receive the benefit of additional security and privacy protection, which are important in a school setting.

Does Google Classroom Contain Ads?

No. Just like the services in G Suite for Education, there are no ads in the Classroom.

If Drive Is Disabled on My G Suite For Education Domain, Can I Still Use Classroom?

No. Google Classroom works with Google Docs, Drive and other services from G Suite for Education to help students in submitting work online, and teachers in creating and collecting assignments. If Drive is disabled, Google Docs and other services will also be disabled. The students will also not be able to put attachments in their work. You will still be able to use the Classroom, but the set of features will be very limited.

Does Google Own the Teacher, Student, Or School Information In The Classroom?

No, Google does not assume ownership of any data of the users in G Suite core services, which include the G Suite for Education. If the school, education department, or the university decides to stop using Google, it is easy for them to take their data with them.

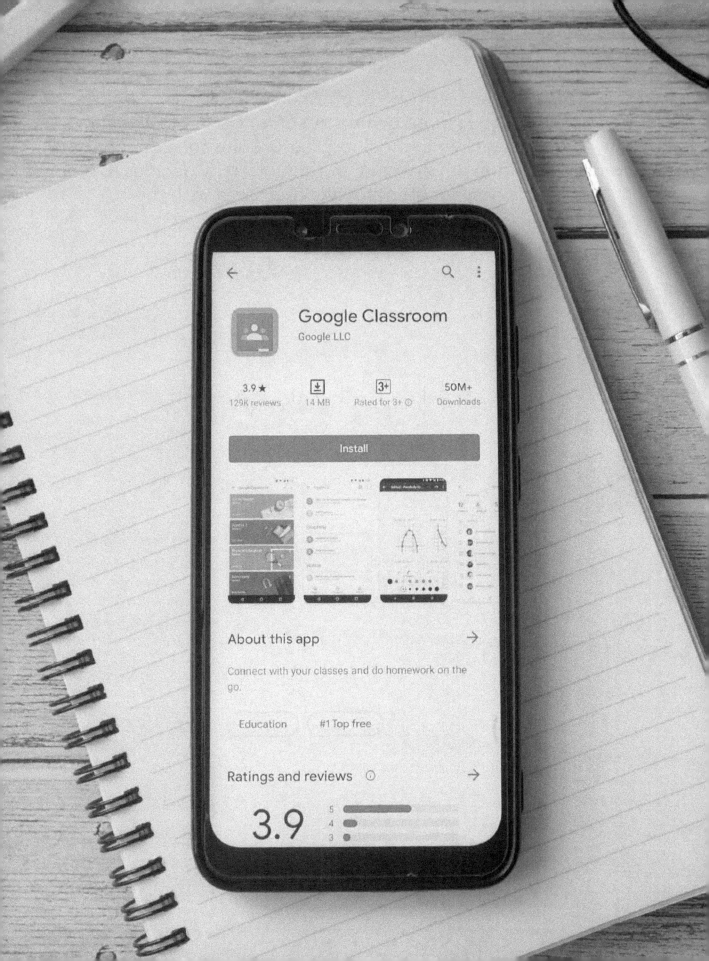

CONCLUSION

So, you have read this book and have some concepts about using Google Classroom. Congratulations on taking strides to enhance your students' education and experiences in your classroom! Comprehending brand-new innovation and its capabilities is an exceptional way to begin.

We have shown you how Google Class can assist you to do so a lot more, in regard to linking students with resources, developing engaging and motivating guidelines, and creating your classroom for partnership. This book consists of only fifty ideas for using Google Classroom, but there are numerous more ways this resource is being used.

What more can you do to change and highly enhance the finding out environment for your students? Continue to find out about and promote the usage of academic innovation. Become familiar with the SAMR design (Alternative, Augmentation, Adjustment, Redefinition) of instructional innovation use. If you consistently integrate innovation at the substitution level, consider how you can go up to another level, and begin to redefine and innovate what learning can look like for students.

Above all, never let your teaching end up being static or routine. Continue to explore ways to improve and sharpen your mentor skills. As the stating goes: school is never out for the professional.

Nowadays in the era of the pandemic, it has become more than ever important to think about a smart solution to organize the rapport between teachers and students; a solution that will help both of them to communicate in an effective way.

Original coverage enables educators and students to see the parts and sections of the research submitted, which includes the same or identical language to that of another source. This shows inadequate quote root resources and flags for students, to help the learner improve their understanding.

Teachers should also show the original chart, so they can check the student's intellectual credibility of the study. Teachers will switch three assignments on G Suite for Education (free) to record originality. This restriction is eliminated on the G Suite for Enterprise in Education (paid). The classroom offers the opportunity for students to record lessons at the end of a term or year. If a lesson is archived, it is deleted from the internet, and put in the preserved classes field to help teachers maintain their current class structure. Once a lesson is stored, instructors and students can view it, so it will not be allowed to make any improvements unless it is updated.

The devices enable users to take photos and attach them to their tasks, move data from other programs, and supports for offline access. As with Google's web apps, Google Classroom does not show advertisements for pupils, faculty, and teachers in its software as part of G Suite for Education, and user details are not scanned for or used for advertisement purposes.

Distance learning has come a long way over the years, with the sole purpose of bringing education to your doorstep, giving anyone who has the basic knowledge of the internet access to the best of education, available anywhere in the world. Before this innovation, it was usual for you to either quit or pause your ongoing engagement to get a new degree. But now you can be engaged and still get a degree, and a good one at that. So, distance learning has been much of a blessing. The concept and idea of distance learning will not work unless there are tools to facilitate it, tools such as Google Classroom, Apple Classroom, etc. Hence this book was written to enlighten and show you the path to follow in creating your own virtual classroom, but our focus was the Google Classroom.

Everything you need to know about the Google Classroom has been revealed in detail, but it is not without flaws and concerns. One such concern is security. This is an issue with any online program since cybercriminals are always in search of data. The data of students and teachers or users of Google Classroom has been taken as a top priority, as the developers keep upgrading their system every month, not only to provide you with the best of experience but to provide you with top-notch security of your data. This book reveals all the steps you need to take, and also the full benefits each feature provides, to give you the best virtual learning experience through Google Classroom.

If you have never used a computer before, or you have not attempted any online class before, no problem, in front of you lies the key to your amazing online learning experience. This book also equips teachers with all they require to manage a Google Classroom, and even guardians are not left.

Google Classroom is accessible from any desktop or mobile device, irrespective of software, through Google Chrome. The classroom introduces the students to an electronic learning program. Teachers and students do not have to shuffle large volumes of paper because the Classroom is paperless.

The classroom period is fine. Teachers and students are allowed to send notes, post to the internet, provide private feedback to assignments, and receive job information. Teachers are totally in control of students' feedback and updates.

Thank you!

www.ingramcontent.com/pod-product-compliance
Lightning Source LLC
La Vergne TN
LVHW081346050326
832903LV00024B/1343